Social Development Activities for Circle Time:
Family and Community

Ages 3-6

by
Cindy Barden

Published by Totline® Publications
an imprint of
Frank Schaffer Publications®

Totline® PUBLICATIONS ™

Author: Cindy Barden
Editor: Mary Rose Hassinger
Interior Designer: Good Neighbor Press, Inc.

Frank Schaffer Publications®

Totline Publications is an imprint of Frank Schaffer Publications.

Send all inquiries to:
Frank Schaffer Publications
8720 Orion Place
Columbus, Ohio 43240-2111

Social Development Activities for Circle Time: Family and Community—Ages 3–6

ISBN: 1-57029-525-5

2 3 4 5 6 7 8 9 10 PAT 10 09 08

Table of Contents

Table of Contents

Social Development Activities for Circle Time: Family and Community

Social Development Activities for Circle Time: Family and Community provides resources for helping young children explore social concepts including friends, families, and communities. Skill-building activities invite children to learn about the people and places they see every day.

The circle time activities in this book include songs, chants, rhymes, and poems. Children brainstorm together, role-play, dramatize stories and scenarios, pantomime, play games, share story time, categorize, compare and contrast, and complete group art activities.

Activities address many of the standards set forth by the National Association for the Education of Young Children (NAEYC) and National Council for Social Studies (NCSS) and can be used as a supplement to your social studies curriculum. A list of preschool social studies goals is included on the next page.

You will find several lists of recommended books on various topics to help you provide children with interesting, colorful, age-appropriate books in your learning center. Change the books every week or two to keep interest high and to tie in with the current topics. In addition, prop box suggestions help you enhance the social studies topics.

Activity pages include materials needed, directions for preparation, and step-by-step instructions for the activity. Frequently you will find ideas for variations and extension activities. Because the attention span of young children is very short, most activities can be done in 10 minutes or less. Longer ones can be broken into smaller units and used over the course of several days.

This book is roughly divided into sections to include Friends, Families, Communities, and Following Rules. Specific activities address how friends, families, and communities change; patriotism; multicultural homes and families; similarities and differences among people; why we have rules; and why following rules is important for members of a group as small as a family or as large as the global community of Earth. Use the activities in any order to best meet your curriculum needs.

Social Studies for Young Children

Many children under the age of six have had little or no experience interacting in social groups larger than the immediate family. Some may have had preschool or day care experience with sharing and cooperating. Others may be children with little or no experience with peer groups.

Social studies expectations for children in this age group include learning to:

★ make friends
★ be a friend to others
★ recognize positive traits in others
★ develop positive traits in themselves
★ appreciate differences in people
★ realize that people have different likes and needs
★ learn about their own families
★ learn the responsibilities of family members
★ get along with family members
★ recognize different types of families
★ understand that people/families/neighborhoods change
★ show respect for others
★ show respect for property
★ recognize and identify with various groups such as a class, a neighborhood, a community, etc.
★ become a participating member of a larger group, such as a class, neighborhood, and community
★ recognize what it takes to be a good neighbor
★ understand that they are also a part of larger communities, such as cities, states, and countries as well as Earth's global community
★ be sensitive to the needs of others
★ interact cooperatively with others
★ acquire basic mapping skills
★ follow rules
★ understand the reason why we have rules
★ practice sharing and cooperating in non-threatening situations
★ learn about different types of homes
★ recognize that people provide goods and services
★ appreciate the diversity of people
★ differentiate between wants and needs

1-57029-525-5 *Social Development Activities for Circle Time: Family and Community*

The Importance of Circle Time

Circle time serves an important role in the development of social skills for young children and is an essential part of early childhood programs. Through circle time, young children can participate in pleasurable learning experiences in a non-threatening, low-risk environment.

Because mistakes are not consequential, circle time gives young children an opportunity to learn how to be part of a group, interact with one another, take turns, develop listening skills, experience music and movement, and play games.

Circle time also provides opportunities for exploring new concepts and practicing social skills such as sharing and cooperating. Children can make new friends, get to know their classmates better, and participate in brainstorming and other activities that inspire creativity. Other benefits include increased levels of self-confidence, enhanced communications, great social awareness, and an increased ability to empathize.

Encourage everyone to participate in circle time, but recognize that some children take longer than others to be comfortable as active participants in a group.

Invite children to join you in a circle time activity by getting their attention. You can do this by softly beating a tom-tom, shaking a tambourine, or singing a short song. Repeat the song several times until everyone has gathered. Change the method about once a month.

Encourage those who arrive first to join you in the song. Children enjoy repetition, so use the same song consistently. Here's an example of a short song you can sing to the tune of "The Farmer in the Dell."

Get ready for circle time
Get ready for circle time
Heigh, ho, it's time, you know.
Get ready for circle time.

At the beginning of the year, set the ground rules for circle time. Write the rules on signs and include a picture showing the rule. Gently remind children who forget the rules by pointing to the appropriate picture. For example: Sit quietly and listen when someone is speaking. Wait your turn. One at a time.

Whether your objective is to introduce a new concept or review what children have already learned, remember . . .

Keep it simple.
Keep it short.
Have fun!

1-57029-525-5 *Social Development Activities for Circle Time: Family and Community*

Recommended Books About Friends for Your Learning Center

Friendship

Amigo by Byrd Baylor

Charlie the Caterpillar by Dom DeLuise

Children Just Like Me by Barnabas and Anabel Kindersley

Chrysanthemum by Kevin Henkes

Corduroy by Don Freeman

Frog and Toad Are Friends (and other Frog and Toad Stories) by Arnold Lobel

Friends at School by Rochelle Bunnett

Gilberto and the Wind by Marie Hall Ets

Happy Birthday, Dear Duck by Eve Bunting

Ira Sleeps Over by Bernard Waber

Jamaica's Find by Juanita Havill

Just My Friend and Me by Mercer Mayer

My Friend Isabelle by Eliza Woloson

A Rainbow of Friends by P.K. Hallinan

That's What a Friend Is by P.K. Hallinan

Toot and Puddle: The New Friend by Holly Hobbie

Will I Have a Friend? by Marian Cohen

Similarities and Differences

Everybody Cooks Rice by Nora Dooley

It's OK to Be Different by Todd Parr

The Sissy Duckling by Hardy Fierstein

The Sneetches by Dr. Seuss

Prop Box Suggestions

Dolls and stuffed figures that represent babies, children, and adults

Items for "playing house" such as furniture, plastic dishes, and toy appliances

Ethnic costumes

"Dress-up" clothes, shoes, hats, and purses for role playing

Puppets or dolls representing a variety of ages and ethnic backgrounds

Welcome Song

(Sing to the tune of "Are You Sleeping?")

Help children get to know you and each other at the beginning of the year by sharing this circle time "Welcome Song."

Sing "Welcome Song" to introduce yourself and tell the children something about you. Children take turns singing, substituting their own names.

Welcome Song

I am (your name).
I am (your name).

How do you do?
How do you do?

I like (name one or two things you like).
I like (name one or two things you like).

I'm glad to meet you.
I'm glad to meet you.

Example: I am Mr. Jones.

Action: Bow or curtsey to the group.

Example: I like dogs and snowstorms.

Action: Smile and shake a child's hand.

At the end of the song, bow to one of the students and ask that child to sing the song using her own name and something she likes. Continue around the circle until everyone has a turn.

Welcome new students who join the class later in the year by singing "Welcome Song." After you and the other children sing your introductions, ask the newest student to do the same.

 # I Have Two Eyes

(Sing to the tune of "The Wheels on the Bus")

Gather children in a circle. Ask everyone to stand. Sing the first verse, substituting the appropriate words describing you. When you get to the last line, motion to a specific child.

Help that child sing the same verse, substituting the words describing her. She motions to another standing child on the last line. When she finishes, she sits down and the next child selected repeats the activity.

Continue until all children are sitting.

Start over with the second verse, substituting with appropriate words. Children can remain sitting, and then stand up after they finish their turns.

Repeat for verse 3 until everyone is sitting again.

I Have Two Eyes

Verse 1:
I have two eyes and they are (blue),
They are (blue); they are (blue),
I have two eyes and they are (blue).
How about you?

Verse 2:
I have (long) hair and it is (red),
It is (red); it is (red),
I have (long) hair and it is (red).
How about you?

Verse 3:
I like (pizza and kangaroos),
(Kangaroos, kangaroos),
I like (pizza and kangaroos).
How about you?

Friends

By Crystal Bowman

A friend is someone who listens,
A friend is someone who cares.
A friend is someone who understands,
A friend is someone who shares.

It's nice to have a special friend
To tell your secrets to.
It's nice to know that someone you like
Is someone who really likes you.

A friend is someone you call on the phone
To talk about nothing at all.
A friend is someone who cheers you up
And makes you feel ten feet tall.

Everyone likes to have
A special friend, it's true.
But if you want a special friend,
You need to be one too.

This song is a great way to begin a circle time discussion of what people can do to make friends with others.

Friends Acrostic: A Circle Time Poem

F
R
I
E
N
D
S

At circle time, write the word FRIENDS in uppercase letters on chart paper in a column, one letter to each line.

Ask children to brainstorm for ideas of words or phrases that begin with each letter in the word. Have the group agree on the best word or phrase for each letter and write it on the appropriate line to create a class acrostic poem.

Use this circle time idea for other group acrostic poems for other words, like *families, love, mother, father,* etc.

1-57029-525-5 *Social Development Activities for Circle Time: Family and Community*

I Have a Friend-O

Welcome children by singing a personalized song as they join you at circle time.

Substitute the child's name for the one given. If the name has more or less than five letters, adjust as needed. See the sample for someone with a short name.

I Have a Friend-O

I have a friend.
Her is name is Erica.
Erica is her name–O.
E-R-I-C-A.
E-R-I-C-A.
E-R-I-C-A.
And Erica is her name-O.

I have a friend.
His name is Bob.
Bob is his name–O.
B-O-B spells Bob.
B-O-B spells Bob.
B-O-B spells Bob.
And Bob is his name-O.

What Makes Someone a Friend?

You will need:

★ Several copies of *Gingerbread Friend Pattern* (decorated if desired)

As a group, encourage children to talk about what makes someone a friend. As they brainstorm for ideas, ask them to name words and phrases that describe friends.

Ask them to give examples from books you've read together at story time or movies they know, like *Charlotte's Web*. (How was Charlotte a good friend to Wilbur?)

Write their words and phrases in colorful markers on the Gingerbread Friends.

Display the Gingerbread Friends on a "Friendship" bulletin board, linked hand to hand.

Extension:

★ Give each child a copy of *Gingerbread Friend Pattern* to cut out and color. Help children write their names on their Gingerbread Friends. Display them on the bulletin board, linked hand to hand.

Gingerbread Friend Pattern

13

1-57029-525-5 *Social Development Activities for Circle Time: Family and Community*

 # I Have Two Hands

(Sing to the tune of "The Wheels on the Bus")

Use this song to reinforce the idea that basically, people are alike.

Gather children in a circle. Sing each verse to the group. Repeat two or three times. Encourage children to join in singing the words and completing the actions.

I Have Two Hands

Words	Actions
I have two hands to shake, shake, shake, Shake, shake, shake; shake, shake, shake, I have two hands to shake, shake, shake On a Monday morning.	Shake hands with various children.
I have two arms to hug my friends, Hug my friends, hug my friends, I have two arms to hug my friends On a Tuesday morning.	Hug a child or a large stuffed animal.
I have two eyes to wink at you, Wink at you, wink at you, I have two eyes to wink at you On a Wednesday morning.	Wink.
I have a mouth to smile at you, Smile at you, smile at you, I have a mouth to smile at you On a Thursday morning.	Smile.
I have two feet to dance a jig, Dance a jig, dance a jig, I have two feet to dance a jig, On a Friday morning.	Dance.

Note: If a verse is inappropriate and might embarrass a child with a disability in your classroom, skip that verse or substitute different words of your own.

Show Me Your Favorite Color

Show children that individual differences are normal and acceptable.

You will need:

★ A large pile of colored blocks, chips, game markers, etc.—any type of manipulative as long as the items are the same shape and size and come in a large variety of colors

★ A large plastic bowl or other type of container

Place the colored manipulatives in a pile in the center of the circle next to the empty container.

Ask each child to take one manipulative in her favorite color from the pile, name the color, and place it in the container.

When everyone has added one manipulative, point out how there are many different colors in the container. That's because people are different. Not everyone likes the same color.

Name Your Favorites

Ask children during circle time for other suggestions about things that people like that are different. As they offer suggestions (different favorite foods, animals, flowers, seasons, books, clothing, etc.) go around the circle and ask each child to name his favorite in that category.

A Friendship Circle

You will need:

★ Colored links or large colored paper clips

While gathered together for circle time, select one colored link or paper clip in your favorite color. Say, "My favorite color is . . ."

Hand the link (or paper clip) to the child next to you. Ask that child to select a link in his favorite color and add the link to yours. Ask the child to say, "My favorite color is . . ."

Continue around the circle having each child add one link and name her favorite color.

When the chain gets back to you, connect the ends to form a circle. Point out how even though we like different colors, they all connect to form one circle.

15

1-57029-525-5 *Social Development Activities for Circle Time: Family and Community*

Outdoor Circle Time

You will need:

★ Chalk (or large sheets of paper and crayons)

If it's a nice day, move circle time outside. Draw a large circle on the playground with chalk. If you can't go outside, use crayons and a large piece of butcher paper or art paper.

Divide the circle your drew into six or eight sections. Label each section with a different option or draw pictures to represent the choices. (Numbers, pets, fruits, games, etc.)

Read or name the word or picture in each section of the circle. Let children take turns making one tally mark in the section of the circle that represents their favorite option.

Have children count together to learn which choice was the group's favorite.

Erase and repeat with other choices.

 # Hands of Friendship

Hold circle time around a table covered with newspaper to complete this cooperative art project.

You will need:

★ Washable paints in five to ten different colors
★ A large piece of poster board
★ Shallow plastic containers large enough for children to place one hand in, palm down (Disposable plastic plates would work.)
★ A roll of paper towels for cleanup

Place a large sheet of poster board in the center of the table.

Ask children to take turns placing one hand in one of the plates of paint and making a hand print on the poster board. Demonstrate how to do this without being tooooo messy.

Have children brainstorm for a friendship-related title for the artwork.

Write the title in colored marker on the poster and display it on the outside of your classroom door for all to see.

Pass on a Hand Hug

At the beginning of circle time, ask children to join hands with you and each other in a circle. Gently squeeze the hand of one of the children next to you. Tell that child you've just given her a "hand hug." Ask her to pass it on by gently squeezing the hand of the child next to her. Let children continue around the circle until the "hand hug" gets back to you.

Use this activity at the beginning of any circle time activity, especially if one of the children looks a bit sad.

Encourage children to start a "hand hug" exchange when they feel the need for a friend.

Musical Chairs Mean Musical Shares

You will need:

★ Half as many chairs as there are students, arranged in a row

Before you gather children for circle time, play music and have them walk around the chairs. When the music stops, children sit on the nearest chair, two to a chair. If you have an odd number of students, you can participate too, so no one is left out. Tell children that they will be partners with the one who shares the chairs for circle time today.

Welcome a New Classmate

Being the "new kid" in class can be frightening. If you know in advance that a new student will be joining your class, let the other children plan ways to make the child feel welcome.

Ask each child to name one thing he could do to make a new child welcome.

You can also use this idea when planning for a guest to your class. This is a great opportunity to emphasize the importance of good manners.

17

1-57029-525-5 *Social Development Activities for Circle Time: Family and Community*

 # Make a Friendship Quilt

To wrap up a unit on friendship, invite children to make a friendship quilt.

You will need:

★ One copy of the quilt block below for each student
★ Crayons, paints, or markers
★ Clear tape

Cut out copies of the quilt block for each child. The quilt will be more interesting if you copy the blocks on different colored construction paper. Ask them to draw a picture of themselves and a friend doing something together in the block. Remember that a friend might be a four-legged one.

At circle time, help them arrange the drawings to form a quilt pattern. If you have an odd number of students, encourage children to make more than one drawing or do some yourself so it comes out even. Turn the papers over and tape together from the back with clear tape. Display in your classroom as a Friends' Day decoration.

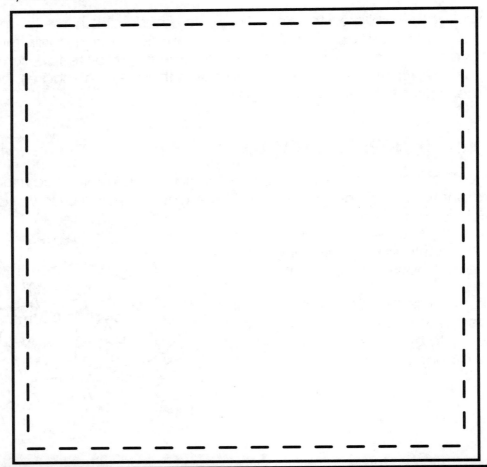

Friends' Day

Hold a Friends' Day in your classroom by planning several circle time activities the children can share with friends of any age.

Let children use some of their circle time to join in planning for Friends' Day. Welcome and use as many of their ideas as possible.

Ask children for suggestions about decorations they could make ahead of time, books you could read together on Friends' Day, games to play, snacks they could share with friends, and invitations for the event.

Remind children that they can invite friends who are older, younger, or the same age.

Encourage children to bring a favorite stuffed animal, action figure, or doll on Friends' Day and introduce it to their school friends.

Hold your Friends' Day as an open house so people can come at times that are most convenient for them.

Plan Games

Plan active cooperative games like a three-legged race, as well as quiet sit together and read a book time. Hold some of your activities in the gym or outside if the weather is cooperative.

Make Visitors Feel Welcome

Assign some of the children to take turns being people greeters.

Have children make friendship necklaces ahead of time and place these around the necks of visitors as they arrive. (See directions on the following page.)

Provide Nametags

Let children help prepare nametags for visitors cut out and decorated in a variety of shapes. On each nametag, print:

MY NAME IS _____.

I AM _____ 'S FRIEND.

1-57029-525-5 *Social Development Activities for Circle Time: Family and Community*

 # Friends' Day (continued)

Make a Friendship Chain

Cut strips of construction paper about 1 inch wide and 8 inches long. As visitors arrive, ask them to write their names on one strip. Form loops to make a paper chain of friendship to display in your classroom. Add it to a chain made earlier by the class.

Plan Entertainment

Include a performance like a class song or dance. Invite visitors to sing or dance along.

Make a Welcome Banner

Create a Welcome banner as part of a circle time art project. Write the word *Welcome* in huge letters on a large piece of art paper or butcher paper. Let children work together to decorate the banner with paints, crayons, or markers.

Decorate

Complete the "Hands of Friendship" activity on page 16 and display the poster on the door. Decorate the room with Gingerbread Friends from that activity.

Friendship Necklaces

Children can help each other make friendship necklaces as a circle time group activity.

You will need:

★ Colored yarn cut into 24" lengths (long enough to go over an adult's head with room to tie the ends together)
★ Disposable paper cups or cupcake cups with about 20 pieces of fruit-flavored, O-shaped cereal for each child

Prepare the strings for the necklaces by putting one piece of cereal on the string and tying a knot around it to hold it on and keep other pieces from slipping off. Leave a few inches of yarn to tie it into a circle when the necklace is finished. Wrap a piece of tape around the other end of the yarn to form a "needle."

Remind children to wash their hands before touching food.

While they are working, tell children that in Hawaii, people give visitors strings of beautiful flowers to welcome them.

Learning About Each Other

You will need:

★ One 3" x 5" index card for each student

Make sets of cards by writing the same number or letter on two cards. For example, write an uppercase A on two cards, an uppercase B on two cards, etc.

At circle time, give each child one of the cards. Hand out cards so that children are paired up with classmates other than the ones they normally sit near.

Go around the circle and ask each child a different question, such as, "Where do you most like to sit and read a book?" or "What is your favorite thing to do on a Saturday?" Make positive comments about their answers. (Oh, I didn't know you liked that! or That's really interesting!)

Explain that when we ask questions and LISTEN to the answers, we learn about each other.

Have children turn to their partner and ask two questions of each other. Then go around the circle again. This time ask each child to name something new he learned about his partner.

Note: Using pairs of cards when asking children to pair up may prevent hurt feelings and allows children to pair up with different classmates rather than their usual "best friends."

Frog and Toad

You will need:

★ *Frog and Toad Are Friends* by Arnold Lobel

Read *Frog and Toad Are Friends* to the children at circle time.

Draw a large Venn diagram on the board or chart paper. Label one side "Frog", one side "Toad", and the center where the circles overlap "Frog and Toad."

Fill in the Venn diagram as children brainstorm for ideas about how Frog and Toad were alike and different.

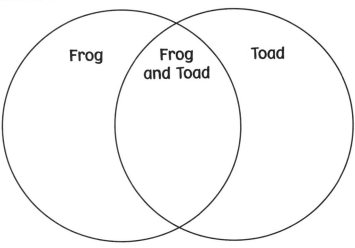

21

1-57029-525-5 *Social Development Activities for Circle Time: Family and Community*

Friends Can Be Different

Follow up a reading of *Frog and Toad Are Friends* or one of the other books in the Frog and Toad series by Arnold Lobel by sharing this rhyming chant with the children at circle time. Encourage them to join in on the last line of each verse.

I Like My Friend and My Friend Likes Me

I have red hair. My friend's hair is brown.
He lives in the country. I live in a town.
But there's one thing we both agree:
I like my friend and my friend likes me.

My friend likes winter. I like summer better.
It's OK that we like different weather.
Because there's one thing we both agree:
I like my friend and my friend likes me. *(Say together)*

I'm good at skating. My friend can ride a bike.
We both like swimming and going on a hike.
And there's another thing we both agree:
I like my friend and my friend likes me. *(Say together)*

I like blue best. My friend says green
Is the best color she's ever seen.
But there's one thing we both agree:
I like my friend and my friend likes me. *(Say together)*

I have a puppy. My friend has a cat.
I wear a cap. She wears a cowboy hat.
It's OK if we don't always agree:
I like my friend and my friend likes me. *(Say together)*

I am short. My friend is tall.
But that doesn't matter. Not at all.
Because there's one thing we both agree:
I like my friend and my friend likes me. *(Say together)*

1-57029-525-5 *Social Development Activities for Circle Time: Family and Community*

A Song of Opposites

(Sing to the tune of "Twinkle, Twinkle Little Star")

Share this friendship song with children at circle time to introduce a lesson about how people can be very different, but still be friends.

We're Great Friends

Let's sing a song of friends we know.
Some run fast and some walk slow.
Some are young and some are old.
Some are timid; some are bold.
We may be different, but that's OK.
We're great friends in every way.

Friends are short and friends are tall.
The bald ones have no hair at all.
Some have brown skin; some do not.
Some wear shirts with lots of dots.
We may be different, but that's OK.
We're great friends in every way.

Friends Come in Many Shapes and Sizes

Use questions like these at circle time to help children realize that friends come in all shapes and sizes.

After each answer, call out, "Let's give a cheer for friends! Hooray!"

Do all friends look alike?
Can friends be younger?
Can friends have brown hair? Red hair?
   Blond hair? Black hair?
Can friends be bald?
Can friends be neighbors?
Can friends be short?
Can friends have four legs?

Can friends be the same age as us?
Can friends be older?
Can friends wear glasses?
Can friends live far away?
Can friends be tall?
Can a shark be a friend?

What Can You Do?

You will need:

★ *Mr. Brown Can Moo, Can You?* by Dr. Seuss

Be prepared for a tangled tongue and lots of giggles as you read *Mr. Brown Can Moo, Can You?* to the group at circle time.

Remind children that Mr. Brown can do many wonderful things and they can too. There are lots of things they can do.

Go around the circle and say to each child, "Mr. Brown can moo. What is something you can do?" Ask each child to tell you something he can do. Be enthusiastic and praise each child for whatever he can do.

Can You?

Recite this poem to children. Then talk about how each of us has different talents. That's what makes us all great.

Can You?

Can you swim in a lake?
Can you bake a cake?
Can you drive a plane
Like my Great-Aunt Jane?

Can you paddle a boat?
Can you bleat like a goat?
Can you rollerskate
Like my cousin Kate?

Can you plant some seeds?
Can you pull some weeds?
Can you ride a bike
Like my good friend, Mike?

Can you tie your shoe?
Can you cook beef stew?
Can you make honey
Like the buzzing bees do?

Can you build a house?
Can you catch a mouse?
Can you tame a lion
Like my Uncle Ryan?

Can you touch your toes?
Can you grow a rose?
Can you climb a tree
Like my Grandpa Lee?

Can you dance a jig?
Can you catch a pig?
Can you play a song
On a drum or a gong?

Can you make a wish?
Can you catch a fish?
Can you ski down a hill
Like my cousin Bill?

Recommended Books About Families for Your Learning Center

Families

ABC: A Family Alphabet Book by Bobbie Combs

All Families Are Different by Sol Gordon

All Kinds of Families by Norma Simon

Annie and the Old One by Miska Miles

Are You My Mother? by P.D. Eastman

The Day We Met You by Phoebe Koehler

Dumpling Soup by Jama Kim Rattigan

Families by Ann Morris

Families by Debbie Bailey

The Family Book by Todd Parr

Fathers, Mothers, Sisters, Brothers: A Collection of Family Poems by Mary Ann Hoberman

Grandfather and I by Helen Buckley

Grandfather's Lovesong by Reeve Lindbergh

Grandma According to Me by Karen Bell

Heather Has Two Mommies by Leslea Newman

I'm a Big Sister and *I'm a Big Brother* by Joanna Cole.

Just Me and My Mom; Just Me and My Dad; Just Grandma and Me; Just Grandpa and Me; This Is My Family all by Mercer Mayer

Julius, The Baby of the World by Kevin Henkes

Masai and I by Virginia Kroll

Over the Moon: An Adoption Tale by Karen Katz

Shoes from Grandpa by Mem Fox

William's Doll by Will Pene du Bois

Who's in a Family? by Robert Skutch

Prop Box Suggestions

Dolls, puppets, and stuffed figures that represent people of different ages and ethnic backgrounds

Dollhouses and furniture

Ethnic costumes

"Dress-up" clothes, shoes, hats, and purses for role playing

We're Not All the Same

Help children understand that although people in a family may not agree on everything, they still love each other. This poem can introduce a circle time activity on families.

We're Not All the Same

My family is great,
But we're not all the same.
Mom likes to read books.
I like to play games.

Dad's hair is short.
Mine is quite long.
Mom plays the tuba.
I sing along.

I really like lizards,
But dad says, "No pets."
I like when it rains
Sister hates to get wet.

I like to sleep late.
Dad gets up so early.
My hair is straight.
My brother's is curly.

Mom drinks coffee.
Dad likes tea.
We all like milk
And cookies, you see.

My family is different,
From one another.
We're not the same,
But we do love each other.

Families Share

Families share. Families care.
When you need them, families are there.
Families can play the whole day long.
Families say, "I'm sorry," when things go wrong.
Families share. Families care.
When you need them, families are there.

How Many?

Sing this song together at circle time. Have students hold up the appropriate number of fingers to answer the questions, even if the answer is none.

Repeat, substituting *girls, pets, grandpas, grandmas, aunts, uncles,* etc., for the word *boys.*

How many boys are in your family?
In your family? In your family?
How many boys are in your family?
Hold up your hand and show me please.

Make Family Puppets

Make and decorate puppets to represent a variety of family members for your prop box and for students to use in role-playing activities during circle time. You can make simple puppets by drawing faces and decorating brown lunch bags to represent people. Glue on plastic eyes or buttons for eyes and noses. Add colored yarn for hair.

Another option is to cut pictures of people from old magazines and glue them on light cardboard. Tape a paint stirrer or craft stick to the back of each one to make simple puppets.

Families Can Be Different

You will need:

★ One copy of *Show Me Your Family Patterns* page

Cut apart the eight representations of families from the *Show Me Your Family Patterns* page. Tape each one to a wall in a row slightly higher than the tallest child.

If you know the numbers of adults and children in any of the children's families are not included, make an appropriate representation for those families. For example, a child's family may include more than two adults or more than four children. Put up at least one blank page in case you need to quickly represent another type of family.

Begin with children in a circle. Ask children to look at the pictures of families. Explain that the taller figures symbolize adults and the smaller ones stand for children.

Go around the circle. Ask each child to say the number of people in his family, then go and stand by the picture that shows the correct number of adults and children.

Together, count the number of children standing by each picture. Write that number on the picture.

Help children arrange the pictures in order from least to most number of people in the family or from most to least by the number written on each picture.

27

Show Me Your Family Patterns

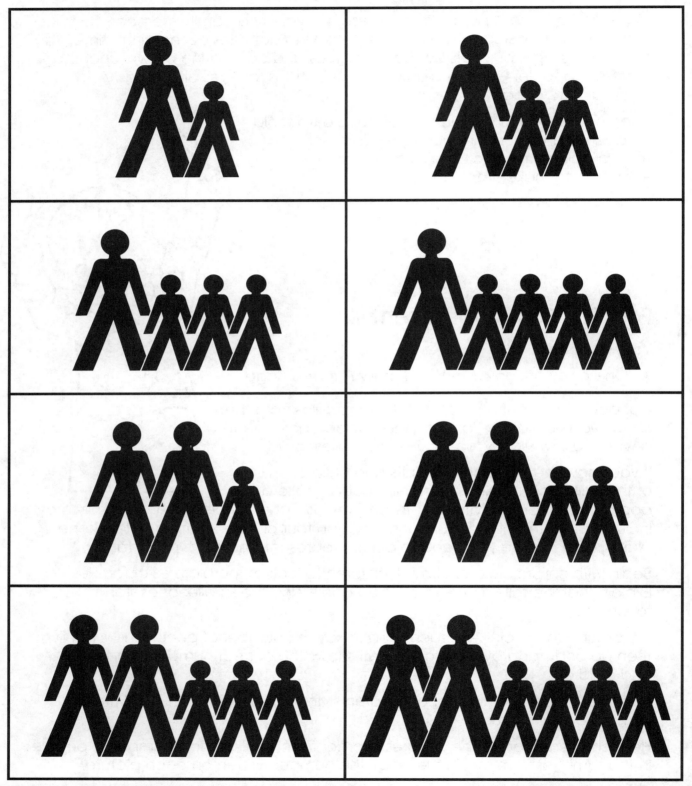

Are You My Mother?

You will need:

★ *Are You My Mother?* by P.D. Eastman

Read *Are You My Mother?* to the children at circle time. Talk about the different animal mothers and babies shown in the book.

Talk about the book by asking questions such as:

Why did the mother bird leave her baby?

How did the baby bird feel when he couldn't find his mother?

Did the mother bird come back for her baby as soon as she could?

Help children differentiate between real and pretend with questions like these:

Do real animals have mothers?

Do machines like cars and airplanes have mothers?

Are You My Mother? Card Game

You will need:

★ A copy of the *Mother and Baby Animal Cards* page

If you'd like larger cards, enlarge the pictures with the copy machine. Copy on light cardboard or laminate the page before cutting out the mother and baby cards.

Give each child an animal baby card at circle time. Keep the mother animal cards on a pile, facedown.

Turn over the mother animal cards, one at a time. Ask a child to name the animal. Then ask, "Who has a baby to go with this mother?"

Place your card and the matching baby animal card faceup in the center of the circle.

Extensions:

★ Let children use the cards for a Memory Game, matching mothers and baby animals.

★ Give each child a copy of the *Mother and Baby Animal Cards* page to color.

Mother and Baby Animal Cards

horse	colt	goose	gosling
duck	duckling	cat	kitten
dog	puppy	rabbit	bunny
hen	chick	pig	piglet
cow	calf	kangaroo	joey
sheep	lamb	bear	cub

1-57029-525-5 *Social Development Activities for Circle Time*
Family and Communit

How Many People Are in Your Family?

You will need:

★ Game markers or chips in two colors, such as red and green

Tell children that red chips stand for boys (and men) and green ones stand for girls (and women).

At circle time, ask children to take turns taking one red chip for each boy in their family; then take one green chip for each girl.

Have children combine the chips into two piles, by color.

Work together to count the number of chips in each pile.

Compare the number of chips in the two piles. Which pile has more chips?

Extend this by using a third color to represent the number of pets.

Let's Talk About Different Kinds of Families

During circle time, encourage a discussion of how families can be different by asking these questions.

Are all families like your family?

Do all families have the same number of adults and children?

Do all families have the same number of boys and girls?

Do all families have the same number of parents, aunts, uncles, grandparents, etc?

Adoption Is a Family Option

You will need:

★ A book about an adopted child: Suggestions include *The Day We Met You* by Phoebe Koehler, *Over the Moon: An Adoption Tale* by Karen Katz, and *I Love You Like Crazy Cakes* by Rose A. Lewis

Children who know they have been adopted may feel that their adoptive parents aren't their "real" parents or feel that they aren't part of the family especially if they look different from their parents. Reading and talking about families with adopted children at circle time as simply another type of family assures children that families come in all shapes, sizes, colors, and combinations.

31

Meet a Member of My Family

In advance, send a letter home with children asking them to bring something to class that reminds them of a member of their family. (Nothing valuable, please.) It could be dad's old fishing hat, a brother's baseball mitt, a sister's stuffed animal, grandmother's favorite book of poems, a baby's blanket . . .

Emphasize that they must have the person's permission for whatever they bring. If children forget to bring something, suggest they go through the prop box for something that reminds them of a family member.

At circle time, ask each child to share what he brought with the group by telling who it belongs to and why the item reminds him of that person. Model this by being the first to share something that belongs to a member of your family.

Families Share Fun Times

Remind children that families share many things. They may share the same house. They may share a bedroom with brothers or sisters. Family members share the chores that need to be done. They also share fun times together.

At circle time, ask each child to describe something fun she likes to do with her family.

Extension:

★ Children can draw or paint pictures of themselves doing something fun with their families and share their drawings with the class at circle time.

Today Is Family Day

Plan a day when children can invite family members to attend school. Set aside an hour or two at the beginning of the day and plan activities to share by people of all ages.

Invite the children and their family members to join you in circle time. (Provide chairs for those who might have trouble getting down on the floor.)

Children can begin circle time by introducing their family members to the group.

Read a favorite book to the group about families. See the list of recommended books on page 25 for suggestions.

Conclude the family day activities by sharing milk or juice and cookies with your visitors.

32

Changes

You will need:

★ *Sky Tree* by Thomas Locker

Read *Sky Tree* to the group at circle time. As you read this lyrical text, encourage children to observe the details of the beautiful illustrations in this glorious celebration of nature and change throughout the seasons. As the tree changes, so does the sky, the ground below the tree, the river, and the mountains in the background.

When you finish, ask questions to encourage a discussion about changes.

How did the tree change?

Even though the tree changed, was it still the same tree?

What other changes happen in our lives? (Day turns to night, seasons change, etc.)

Do people ever change? How? (Children grow up; change what they like to do, or eat, or read; etc.)

Do families always stay the same? Why not?

When a new baby is born, is the baby a member of the family?

If a grandparent or other relative comes to live with you, is that person part of your family?

If a big brother or sister (or parent) moves to different house, are they still part of your family?

If a family member moves far, far away, is that person still part of the family?

What other kinds of changes can happen in a family?

33

Families Can Change

You will need:

★ *Julius, The Baby of the World* by Kevin Henkes
★ Dolls, stuffed animals

Give each child a cuddly doll or stuffed animal.

Read *Julius, The Baby of the World* to the children at circle time. Encourage children to cuddle the dolls and stuffed animals as you read about how Lilly's mother and father kiss their baby's wet pink nose, admire his small black eyes, and stroke his sweet white fur.

After reading, encourage children to talk about how Lilly's family changed when Julius was born.

Talk about how Lilly changed by comparing what she was like when Julius was first born and how she acted at the end of the story.

Big Brothers and Big Sisters Are Important

You will need:

★ *Julius, The Baby of the World* by Kevin Henkes

At circle time, read *Julius, The Baby of the World* if you haven't read it to the students recently.

After reading the book, encourage children to talk about how important it is to be a big brother or big sister. These questions can help get a discussion going.

How many of you have little brothers or sisters?

How can big brothers and big sisters help new babies learn to be clever?

What else can big brothers and sisters do?

Why is being a big brother or big sister so important?

How could you be a good big brother or big sister if you had a baby brother like Julius?

Tell Us More About Your Family

You will need:

★ *Jobs People Do* by Christopher Maynard

Read *Jobs People Do* to the children at circle time.

Talk about the different jobs shown in the story.

Ask each child to ask his mother, father, or another adult about the job he or she does. Suggest they ask questions such as: Where do you work? What do you do there? Do you wear any special clothing or use special equipment?

Follow up at circle time the next day or so by asking volunteers to tell what they learned about the job a member in their family has.

My How Things Have Changed!

Grandparents, great-grandparents, great aunts and uncles, other older adult relatives, and close family friends can be a great source of information for children about families, neighborhoods, and communities in the past.

Send a letter home with children inviting a grandparent or older relative or neighbor to school to celebrate Grandparents Week. Set up a day and time for that person to visit the class. If possible, ask one of your older relatives to visit also.

At circle time, ask the child to introduce his guest. Ask the guest to tell the group something that was very different when she was a child. (Remind guests that children have short attention spans, so they will be asked to talk for only five or ten minutes at most.) If the guest is from a different country, he may want to tell children about how life was different in that country.

Allow a few minutes for children to ask the guest questions. After circle time, let the child take her guest on a tour of the classroom (or school, if appropriate).

Extension:

★ Take a photo of the guest with the children. Send a copy of the photo to the guest with a group thank-you drawing or letter. (This can lead to a lesson on manners, remembering to say "thank you," and writing a friendly letter.)

Books About Homes and Schools for Your Learning Center

Homes

A House for Birdie by Stuart Murphy

A House for Hermit Crab by Eric Carle

Homeplace by Anne Shelby

Homes Around the World by Bobbie Kalman

A House Is a House for Me by Mary Ann Hoberman

Houses and Homes (Around the World) by Ann Morris

Schools

D.W.'s Guide to Preschool by Marc Brown

Friends at School by Rochelle Bunnett

Going to School by Anne Civardi

Miss Bindergarten Gets Ready for Kindergarten by Joseph Slate

Starting School by Janet Ahlberg

Will I Have a Friend? by Marian Cohen

Prop Box Suggestions

Dollhouses and furniture

Photo album of places in your neighborhood and community

Huge cardboard box (from large appliance) decorated to make a playhouse

The Best Kind of Home for Me

You will need:

★ Illustrations cut from magazine or downloaded from the Internet showing different types of dwellings such as condominiums, single-family homes, duplexes, high-rise apartments, log cabins, mansions, castles, as well as homes from different cultures, such as adobe pueblos, igloos, stilt homes, huts, etc.

Use this short poem at circle time to introduce the idea that different kinds of animals live in different kinds of homes. Like animals, not all people live in the same kinds of homes.

The Best Kind of Home for Me

The fish lives in the river.
The bird lives in the tree.
But a home with a roof and walls
Is best for my family and me.

A bird lives in a nest
High up in a tree,
But a home with a roof and walls
Is best for my family and me.

The bug lives in the bush.
The whale lives in the sea.
But a home with a roof and walls
Is best or my family and me.

A bat lives in a cave
As dark as dark can be,
But a home with a roof and walls
Is best for my family and me.

Show children the pictures of different types of homes. Ask questions to encourage thought and discussion. Here are some examples:

How are animal homes different from people homes?
How are these people homes different?
Why do you think not all homes are alike?
Which of the homes is most like the one where you live?
Which of the homes would you most like to live in with your family?
Which of these homes do you think might be in a different country? Why?

Homes Around the World

You will need:

★ Illustrations of homes from different cultures cut from magazines or downloaded from the Internet

★ Books depicting homes in different countries such as *Homes Around the World* by Bobbie Kalman and *Houses and Homes (Around the World)* by Ann Morris

Share pictures of different types of homes from other countries and cultures during circle time. Encourage children to compare and contrast homes from other cultures with the types of homes in their neighborhood.

Everyone Needs a Home

You will need:

★ One copy of *Animals and Their Homes* cut apart

Note: Use with an even-numbered group of 12 or less (or make additional pairs).

Turn pictures facedown in the middle of the floor at circle time. Have each child take one picture.

Ask each child with an animal picture to name the animal. Have children with animal home pictures show their cards. The child with the animal picture decides which illustration shows the appropriate home for that animal.

Have children place the animal/home pairs together in the middle of the circle.

Talk about why different animals live in different types of homes.

Extensions:

★ Laminate the *Animals and Their Homes* page and cut out the cards. Let children use the cards for a Memory Game.

★ Give each child a copy of the *Animals and Their Homes* page to color.

★ Ask children to draw their homes. Help them to write their addresses on the backs of their drawings.

Animals and Their Homes

1-57029-525-5 *Social Development Activities for Circle Time: Family and Community*

What Can You Find in a Home?

You will need:

★ *In a People House* by Theo Le Sieg.

Read *In a People House* to the children at circle time. Ask children to brainstorm for ideas of what can be found in homes (Besides the obvious: windows, doors, ceilings, floors, etc., encourage children to think of more abstract ideas, like love, family, cooperation, safety, security, etc.).

Our Homes Are Special

You will need:

★ A long piece of butcher paper
★ Glue stick
★ Pictures of a variety of types of homes found in your community: include single-family home, farmhouse, ranch style, two-story, duplex, row house, apartment building, etc. Pictures can be cut from magazines or downloaded from the Internet. Check the "Homes for Sale" section of local newspapers.
★ You could go to **http://www.realtor.com**. Use the map option to locate pictures of homes in your community to print.
★ An alternative would be to actually go around the neighborhood and take photos of homes in the area.

Use a marker to write the words *Our homes are special* in large letters along the bottom of the strip of butcher paper.

At circle time, show children pictures of different homes in the neighborhood to promote a discussion of how different types of homes are the same and how they are different.

Place the pictures in the center of the circle and allow each child to select one picture that looks similar to the home where they live and glue it on to the butcher paper in a long row. Ask each child to write her name under the home she selected.

Display the group picture on the wall or in the hallway outside your classroom.

40

Where Do You Live?

Follow up a lesson on learning addresses and telephone numbers with this circle time activity.

In advance, make a list of each child's address.

At circle time, read the addresses, one at a time in random order. Say, "If you live at 123 Fourth Street, please stand up."

Repeat in random order, this time asking children to sit when they hear their addresses.

Simon Says

In advance, prepare a list of directions based on where children live and the names of family members. Directions should be worded to include as many of the children from the group as possible and something fun they should do. Be certain to include all of the children in several of the directions.

At circle time, have children stand. Explain that when you give a direction, everyone should listen carefully. They should follow the directions only if it relates to them.

Suggested directions and actions

If you have a brother . . .   . . . stand on one leg like a stork.

If you live on First Avenue . . .   . . . hold up your thumbs.

If anyone in your family is named Joe . . .   . . . raise your right hand.

If you have a pet . . .   . . . bark like a dog.

If anyone in your family has curly hair . . . . . . wiggle your eyebrows.

If your home is near a grocery store . . .   . . . pretend to eat a banana.

If you live in an apartment . . .   . . . hop twice like a kangaroo.

If anyone in your family likes pizza . . .   . . . roar like a lion.

In anyone in your family wears glasses . . . . . . walk like a duck.

What Can We Find at Our School?

(Sing to the tune of "London Bridge")

Sing both verses of this song to the children.

What's at Our School?

What can we find around our school?
Around our school,
Around our school.
What can we find around our school?
Tell me what you see.

We see (children) in our school
In our school,
In our school.
We see children in our school.
That's one thing that we see.

Repeat verse 1. At the end of the verse, motion to one child and ask him to answer the question.

Sing the second verse, substituting the name of the item suggested by the child for the word *children*.

Repeat several times until everyone has a turn naming something that belongs in a school. If a child can't think of anything, encourage her to look around the classroom for ideas. Encourage children to join in as they learn the words.

Why Do People Go to School?

Encourage children to brainstorm for reasons why children go to school.

Remind them that adults sometimes go to school too.

Ask: Why do adults go to school?
Are you ever too old to go to school?
Do children and adults go to school for the same reasons?
Do animals go to school?
What kind of school do animals attend?

School Is Great!

Use this short poem at circle time before beginning an activity about school.

School is great!
I can't wait
To go to school each day.
I like reading,
Drawing too.
I can't wait to go to school.

School is great!
I can't wait
To go to school each day.
I like numbers,
Music too.
I can't wait to go to school.

Invite children to add more verses substituting their own words in lines 4 and 5.

Schools Have Rules

Use circle time to discuss what rules schools have and why schools have rules. Talk about how different schools have different rules. (Examples: Some schools require uniforms. Schools for older students have different rules than schools for younger ones.)

Ask volunteers for suggestions of what would be a good rule for all schools? (Examples: Take turns. Listen when someone else is talking. Be polite to each other. Say "please" and "thank you." Sit still in class. etc.)

Classmates Linked Together

This circle time activity reinforces the idea that even though we are individuals, we are also part of a group.

You will need:

★ 8-inch strips of construction paper, about 1 inch wide in several different colors
★ Pencils
★ A stapler

Take one strip of paper and write your name on it. Roll it and staple the ends together to form a loop. Let each child take one strip of paper and write his or her name on it.

Ask children to bring their paper strip to you one at a time. As each one hands it to you, ask the child a question about being a member of the class, such as: What do you like to do best with your classmates? or What's your favorite school activity?

As each child answers, put the child's link through the last one to form another loop. Staple the ends together. Continue until you have added a link for each child. Fasten the two ends together to show that you are one group who works, plays, and learns together.

1-57029-525-5 *Social Development Activities for Circle Time: Family and Community*

This Is the Way . . .

Some days children require a more active circle time activity. Ask children to stand in a circle. Sing this song as children make up actions to go with the words.

Words	Suggested actions
This is the way we go to school; Go to school; go to school; This is the way we go to school On a Monday morning.	Children hold hands and march together until they get back to their original place.
This is the way we greet our friends; Greet our friends; greet our friends; This is the way we greet our friends On a Tuesday morning.	Children turn to each other and wave or shake hands.
This is the way we read a book; Read a book; read a book; This is the way we read a book On a Wednesday morning.	Children sit and pretend to read a book.
This is the way we write our names; Write our names; write our names; This is the way we write our names On a Thursday morning.	Children sit and pretend to write their names.
This is the way we paint a picture; Paint a picture; paint a picture; This is the way we paint a picture On a Friday morning.	Children stand and pretend they are painting at an easel.

Extension:

★ As children go from the classroom to the gym, lunchroom, playground, or other location in the school, sing the above song, substituting the name of the appropriate place and day of the week.

Let's Compare

This circle time activity helps children learn to compare and contrast two places. Ask children to name ways a school is like a house and ways the two places are different.

Draw a large Venn diagram on the board or chart paper. Label one side "Home," one side "School," and the center where the circles overlap "Home and School." Fill in the Venn diagram as children brainstorm for ideas about how the two places are alike and different.

Learning About Maps

You will need:

★ The largest neighborhood, community, or city map available. (You may be able to obtain one from a local transit company or from your city's Chamber of Commerce. Also check your local telephone book for a street map and enlarge it on a copy machine.)

★ Several Web sites such as **http://www.mapquest.com/** allow you to create and print maps of a specific area. If you prefer, draw your own.

★ Toy cars, trucks, miniature plastic figures

Tape the map to the floor in the center of the circle. Help children find your school on the map. Draw pictures on the map to show the location of the school and other familiar buildings and places in your neighborhood. Read street names around your school together. Let children drive their toy cars or walk the plastic figures from the school to other locations in your neighborhood.

Use direction words like *north, south, east, west, left* and *right* as you discuss various places in relation to each other.

A Floor Plan of the Classroom

You will need:

★ A large piece of white poster board or art paper

★ Markers or colored pencils

In advance, measure the classroom and draw the outline of the room to scale, but do not add any details other than the door.

Place the drawing of the room in the middle of the circle. At circle time, talk about how a floor plan is a type of a map. It shows a picture of a smaller area than a city map, such as one building or one room. Explain that you will work together to draw a floor plan of your classroom.

Ask children to take turns suggesting items in your classroom to add to the floor plan, such as windows, desks, tables, the learning center, aquarium, etc. Have that child point out about where on the floor plan the item would be. Draw and label each item on the floor plan.

Extensions:

★ Let children prepare floor plans of their homes or bedrooms.

★ Hide "buried treasure." Make a map of the playground or another room in your school. As a group, children can study the map and find the hidden treasure.

Give a Cheer!

Young children do not have enough experience to identify with a larger social unit such as a city, state, or country. However, they can learn about loyalty and pride in their school.

Ask children if they have ever seen a cheerleader at a basketball or football game. What does a cheerleader do?

Ask them to join in shouting out a cheer for your school. You can make up your own or use one of the ideas below.

Hip, hip, hooray!
We're at school today.
We join our friends
To work and play!
Hip, hip, hooray!

Give me a G
Give me an R
Give me an E
Give me an A
Give me a T
What does it spell?
GREAT!

Extensions:

★ When a child does something particularly noteworthy, mention it at circle time, then do a group cheer by spelling out her name. (Give me a J: Give me an A: Give me an N: What does it spell? JAN! HOORAY!)

★ Children can make up cheers about their families and share them with the group at circle time.

The Best Thing About Our School

At circle time, say, "The best thing about our school is . . ." and finish the sentence. Ask the children to take turns saying what they think is the best thing about their school.

Encourage children to have a positive attitude by asking them to name the "best thing" about people and places. On different days, ask children to finish a different "best thing about" sentence. Suggestions include:

The best thing about my family is . . .
The best thing about my home is . . .
The best thing about my neighborhood is . . .
The best thing about our playground is . . .
The best thing about our library is . . .
The best thing about . . . (name a place they visited on a field trip)

Working Together

(Sing to the tune of "Found a Peanut")

Sing this cooperation song with the children as they work together to put away toys, books, or other items after circle time.

Work together,
Work together,
Work together
Until we're done.
If we quickly work together,
We will have more time for fun.

Jobs Go Quickly When We Cooperate

You will need:

★ A box of blocks or other small items
★ A stopwatch or clock with a second hand

This circle time activity demonstrates how working together saves time and effort. While gathered for circle time, empty a box of blocks on the floor in the middle of the circle.

Ask one of the children to pick up the blocks and put them back in the box. Time the child with a stopwatch. Thank the child and tell the group how long it took one child to do that job.

Ask them what they think would happen if they had all helped pick up the blocks.

Dump the blocks again and time them while they all pick up the blocks. Tell them how much more quickly they were able to get the job done when they all worked together.

Ask children what other jobs would go more quickly if they worked together.

Teach children this short rhyme:

Working together is lots of fun.
It makes work go faster
And gets the job done.
If you help me, and I help you,
There isn't anything we can't do!

 # How Can We Share?

Children learn one of the duties of being a member of a family, class, team, or community when they learn to share.

You will need:

★ Art paper
★ Crayons, markers, paint, or colored pencils

Ask each child to select one item from the classroom to bring to circle time (book, stuffed animal, a box of crayons, a picture, etc.).

Discuss what the word *share* means.

Ask questions like the ones below to encourage children to talk about sharing. Get responses from several volunteers for each question.

Is sharing always easy?

Does everyone like to share?

When don't you like to share?

How do you feel when you share?

How do you feel when others share with you?

How do you feel when others do not share with you?

How do you think others feel when you do not share?

Name items that none of the children have brought to circle time. Ask children to give examples of how they could share each of the items such as a smile, a rainbow, a puppy, a swimming pool, a bag of apples, a new song that they learned, etc.

Ask each child to show the item she is holding and name one way she could share it with a friend. ("Will you show us what you brought to circle time today? How could you share that with a friend?")

Extension:

★ Ask children to draw pictures of themselves showing a time when they shared something with a friend or family member.
★ Ask children to share their drawings during circle time by showing their pictures and describing the sharing event.

Sharing What's in the Mystery Bag

You will need:

★ One brown paper lunch bag for each student
★ A variety of objects that children could share
★ A large laundry basket

In advance, place one small object in each of the bags and tape them shut. Suggestions include a small book, several links, a box of crayons, a small hand puppet, a stuffed animal or doll, one toy car or truck, a deck of cards, a musical instrument, a puzzle, a coloring book, and a small notebook.

Place the lunch bags in the laundry basket in the middle of the circle. Start by reviewing what it means to share.

Ask one child to select one of the lunch bags and remove the object inside. Ask him to show the object to everyone, name what it is, and one way he could share it with friends. If he seems stumped, ask leading questions to help him find an answer. Ask the other children for more ideas on how they could share that object.

When the child finishes, have him set aside the bag and the object.

Children take turns selecting bags and naming ways to share what's inside. You might want to discourage shaking, squeezing, and other attempts to figure out what's inside. Ask children to simply take whichever bag is closest to them.

When circle time is over, ask children to return the objects and bags to the laundry basket for a quick cleanup.

Variation:

★ As each child shows what is in the bag, ask a different specific question, such as:

How could you share that with your brother?
How could you share that with three friends?
How could you share that with a classmate?
How could you share that on a rainy day?
How could you share that at the park?

49 1-57029-525-5 *Social Development Activities for Circle Time: Family and Community*

Stone Soup for the Group

You will need:

★ *Stone Soup* by Marcia Brown
★ A large plastic bowl
★ A wooden spoon
★ A small plastic bowl or cup for each child
★ Sandwich bags of "trail mix" ingredients
★ A large "stone" (This can be any clean, inedible item that can be put in the bowl to start the soup.)

In advance, send a letter home asking parents to send a sandwich bag with some type of finger food such as raisins, dry cereal like Chex™ or Trix™, chow mein noodles, mints, shelled sunflower seeds, animal crackers, dried fruit, or other items that could be used to make a "trail mix." You might want to specify no chocolate or no candy. (Awareness of any student food allergies is a helpful precautionary measure.)

When children arrive, ask them to give you the bags to set aside until later.

If you'd prefer, make up a sandwich bag of trail mix ingredients for each child. (Some children will forget to bring an ingredient, so have a few extra bags on hand, just in case. Then no one will feel left out.)

At snack time, read *Stone Soup* to the class. When you finish, talk about how all the people in the village shared with the soldiers. When everyone shared a little, there was plenty for everyone.

Tell children they are going to make their own stone snack. Take the large bowl and spoon and add one "stone." Tell children the block or other item you use represents the stone used by the soldier to start the stone soup.

Say: "Is our stone snack ready to eat yet?" (Act surprised when they say "no.") "No? How about if we add a few other ingredients?"

Give each child a bag of ingredients. Ask each one to tell what she has and then empty the bag into the large plastic bowl. After adding each ingredient, ask the child to take the wooden spoon and stir it all together.

When all the bags are emptied (don't forget to add one yourself if you want to share in the treat), use the wooden spoon to dish out some of the stone snack for each member of the group.

Be Kind to Others

Introduce children to the "Golden Rule" with this poem.

Be Kind to Others

Treat others the way
You'd want them to treat you
That's what we call
The Golden Rule.

Be kind to others.
Always be polite.
Treat others fairly.
That is always right.

Say, "Excuse me." when you burp.
Say "please" and "thank you" too.
Help your friends and family
And they will help you.

Share a smile. Share a book.
Share a trip to the zoo.
Share with your brothers
And your sisters too.

Treat others the way
You'd want them to treat you
That's what we call
The Golden Rule.

Remember the Golden Rule

Write this rule on a large banner and display it at circle time:

Always treat others the way you would like to be treated.

Read the words. Tell children we call this the Golden Rule. Help children to start thinking about this concept by asking questions at circle time.

Ask: Why is this a good rule for everyone to follow?
Why is this a good rule at home?
Why is this a good rule at school?
Why is this a good rule for people in a neighborhood?
Why is this a good rule for people in a country?

Ask children to brainstorm actions that display how they can follow this rule for each of the above.

1-57029-525-5 *Social Development Activities for Circle Time: Family and Community*

 # What Should You Do?

This circle time activity provides an excellent way to help children understand how they are responsible for their own actions as they visualize themselves as a contributing participant of a group.

Use the ideas over the course of two or more different circle time sessions to maintain children's interest.

Read the situations below one at a time. For each situation, ask, "What should you do?" and "Why?"

Encourage children to share their ideas. For items marked with an *, you could ask the group, "Will you show me what you would do?" rather than asking for a verbal response.

Your mom is having a birthday tomorrow. Your brothers and sister want to plan a party.

Your grandparents ask you to help rake leaves. You don't like to rake leaves.

Your neighbor is carrying a bag of groceries into her house. The bag breaks.

You have five cookies. Your four friends have no cookies.

Your neighbor asks you to turn down the radio. It is loud and she wants to take a nap.

A cousin you don't like comes over to play. Yesterday his dog died.

You and your mom are home together. Your mom has a bad cold and doesn't feel like getting up to make breakfast.

Your dad is working at home today. He asked you to play quietly in your room for a while. You really, really want to go outside and ride your bike.

* Your baby brother drops his bowl of cereal on the floor.

* You mom loses her car keys at the grocery store.

* A classmate spills her box of crayons on the floor and they roll away.

* Your grandfather can't find his glasses.

* Your toys are on the steps. You're in a hurry to go out and play.

* Your dad spills a box of nails in the driveway.

Recommended Books About Communities and Community Helpers for Your Learning Center

Neighborhoods/Communities

Ant Cities by Arthur Dorros

A Chair for My Mother by Verra Williams

Curious George Goes to the Hospital by Margaret and H.A. Rey

Earthdance by Joanne Ryder

Going to the Doctor by Fred Rogers

The Little House by Virginia Lee Burton

My Street by Rebecca Treays

Smoky Night by Eve Bunting

A Visit to the Sesame Street Firehouse by Dan elliott

A Visit to the Sesame Street Library by Deborah Hautzig

A Visit to the Sesame Street Museum by Liza Alexander

Books in the "Magic School Bus" series by Joanna Cole that depict field trips to places in the community, such as *Ready, Set, Dough* and *At the Waterworks*

Community Helpers/Occupations

The Berenstain Bears on the Job, The Berenstain Bears Go to the Doctor, The Berenstain Bears Visit the Dentist by Stan and Jan Berenstain

Clifford the Firehouse Dog by Norman Bridwell

Community Helpers from A–Z by Bobbie Kolman

Fire Fighters to the Rescue by Jack C. Harris

Jobs People Do by Christopher Maynard

Neighborhood Friends by Margaret Johnson

On the Beat by Barry Robinson

What Will I Be?: Dora's Book About Jobs by Phoebe Beinstein

"This Is What I Want to Be" series published by Heinemann Library

Learning About Our Neighborhoods

 # More Recommended Books for Your Learning Center

Being Homeless

A Shelter in Our Car by Monica Gunning

Braids Girl by Lisa McCourt

Gowanus Dog by Jonathon Frost

Multicultural

Dumpling Soup by Jama Kim Rattigan

Gracias: The Thanksgiving Turkey by Joy Crowley

Lion Dancer: Ernie Wan's Chinese New Year by Kate Waters & Madeline Slovenz-Low

Masai and I by Virginia Kroll

Map Reading/Geography

As the Crow Flies by Gail Hartman

Mapping Penny's World by Loreen Leedy

 # Prop Box Suggestions

Hats, badges, or other articles of clothing that represent different occupations

Tools used by different occupations such as a play stethoscope, plastic hammer, shovel, broom, paintbrush, or musical instrument

Toy cars and other types of vehicles

Large building blocks

Cardboard boxes in various shapes and sizes for building

Play mats depicting buildings and streets

Hard hats

Uniforms for dress-up, let's pretend, and role-playing activities

Atlases

City, county, state, road, subway, and street maps

A play doctor or nurse's kit

A real stethoscope

Published by Totline Publications. Copyright Protected.

54

1-57029-525-5 *Social Development Activities for Circle Time: Family and Community*

Field Trip Suggestions

Children enjoy field trips, even if they aren't as exciting as the ones Ms. Fizzle plans. Use circle time to prepare children by teaching them about the place they will visit and as follow-up activities after the field trip. These suggestions may spark ideas for field trips in your community.

Post office	Health spa
Fire station	Police station
Bakery or ice cream store	Grocery store or deli
Apple orchard	Farm
Factory	Ethnic restaurant
Antique store	Pet store
Zoo or petting zoo	Traffic court
Florist	Nursery
Pharmacy	Clinic or hospital
Mall	Veterinarian's office
Kennel	Humane Society
Park	Pro or semipro sports arena
Memorial place or building	Museum of natural history, art, local history

Field Trip Songs

(Sing to the tune of "Here We Go 'Round The Mulberry Bush")

Sing this song with the children at circle time after a field trip to the school library or local library.

Today We Went to the Library

Today we went to the library,

The library, the library.

Today we went to the library

And this is what we saw.

We saw books at the library,

The library, the library.

We saw books at the library.

That is what we saw today.

Encourage children to add additional verses, substituting other words for *books* to describe what they saw.

Extension:

★ Using the above song as a model, modify it to sing with children after a field trip to another location in your neighborhood.

 # Places in Our Neighborhood

You will need:

★ A copy of the three pages of *Places in Our Neighborhood* (Pictures can be cut apart if you'd like.)

★ **Optional:** other pictures cut from magazines or photos of places likely to be found in your community

Ask children to take turns at circle time naming different places they see on their way to school each day. For each place, ask the child to tell something about it. (Irma's Corner Store sells groceries, The Sock Hop Shop sells jump ropes and socks, Green's Garage fixes green cars, The Book Nook sells books and magazines, Lincoln Park is a playground, etc.)

Show each of the pictures of *Places in Our Neighborhood*. Talk about what people might find at each place.

 # Places in Our Neighborhood Game

You will need:

★ Two sets of the three *Places in Our Neighborhood* pages: copy on light cardboard or laminate and cut apart.

Deal out the cards to children at circle time. If there are an odd number of cards, keep those for yourself.

Ask children to look for pairs. If they have two of the same, ask them to place the pairs together in the center of the circle.

Model how to play. Show a card and say, "I have a picture of a bakery. Who has a card to match mine?"

Place your card and the matching card faceup in the center of the circle.

Children take turns showing one of their cards and naming the place, then asking who has a card to match. Continue until all matches are showing.

Extensions:

★ Let children use the cards for a Memory Game.

★ Give each child a copy of the *Places in Our Neighborhood* pages color.

Places in Our Neighborhood Patterns

Places In Our Neighborhood Patterns

Places in Our Neighborhood Patterns

59

1-57029-525-5 *Social Development Activities for Circle Time: Family and Community*

 # Where Would It Be?

Sing each verse. Pause after the words *at the* and let children fill in an answer. Answers are suggested, but for many verses, there can be more than one right answer.

Oh where, oh where would you buy bread and milk?
Buy bread and milk? Buy bread and milk?
Oh where, oh where would you buy bread and milk?
At the grocery store.

Oh where, oh where would you buy postage stamps?
Buy postage stamps? Buy postage stamps?
Oh where, oh where would you buy postage stamps?
At the post office.

Continue with more verses using the ideas below or make up your own.

Oh where, oh where would you . . .

. . . meet with your friends?	(playground or park)
. . . buy a new hat?	(clothing store)
. . . buy new shoes and socks?	(shoe store or clothing store)
. . . buy a new toy?	(toy store)
. . . get new glasses?	(eye doctor)
. . . buy hammer and nails?	(hardware store)
. . . mail a birthday card?	(post office)
. . . buy a ham sandwich?	(deli, restaurant)
. . . rent a video?	(video store, library)
. . . buy a pound of stinky cheese?	(grocery store, deli)
. . . get food for your fish?	(pet store)
. . . buy a new car?	(used car lot)
. . . get gas for your car?	(gas station)
. . . look at great art?	(gallery or museum)
. . . find a good book?	(bookstore, library)
. . . get a broken arm fixed?	(clinic, hospital)
. . . eat Chinese food?	(restaurant)
. . . find a lion that roars?	(zoo)

Around Our Town

You will need:

★ A large neighborhood, community, or city map (You may be able to obtain one from a local transit company or from your city's Chamber of Commerce.)

★ Postcards or photos that show familiar landmarks in your community

★ Pushpins and markers (or colored sticker dots) in different colors

Gather six to ten postcards and photos of various places in your community. You could cut photos from a local newspaper or take your own. Suggestions include your school, familiar buildings like the local post office, library, fire station, police station, etc., as well as lakes, parks, mountains, statues, etc.

Place the map on the floor at circle time.

Ask children to name the city where they live.

Show them the city map and explain that a map is a special kind of picture of a larger area. It's like being high up in the sky and looking down. Help them identify nearby familiar streets.

Show children a photo of your school. As a group, locate your school on the map. Mark it with a blue circle or sticker dot.

Show students the other postcards or photos, one at a time. Help them name the place shown and find its location on the map. Mark each location with a different colored marker or colored sticker dot.

Demonstrate how to go from one location to another by "walking" your fingers from your school to the neighborhood library or swimming pool. Let students take turns showing the way from one specified location to another.

Extension:

★ When you finish, display the map on the bulletin board. Use same-colored pushpins to match the colored circles for displaying the photos next to the map.

This Is the Way We Build a Town

Give children a large assortment of building blocks or other building materials in various colors and sizes. Small cardboard boxes, empty thread spools, or plastic bottles and containers can also be used for building. Encourage them to work together in groups to build homes or other community buildings with blocks to make a class town. This activity encourages cooperation, and planning, as well as dexterity skills.

Let's Create Our Town

Children work together and utilize planning skills as they consider the needs of people in a community and create their own imaginary town.

Consider dividing this activity into smaller units and completing it during several circle time sessions over the course of a week.

You will need:

★ Several feet of butcher paper

★ Tape

★ Crayons and markers

★ Glue sticks

★ Toys cars and other vehicles

★ Scissors

★ Small dolls or plastic figures of people and animals

★ Several copies of *Places in Our Neighborhood* on pages 57–59, cut apart

★ Several copies of *Home Patterns*, cut apart

★ Colored construction paper cut into appropriate-size building shapes (squares, pentagons, rectangles)

★ Books with illustrations of places in a neighborhood such as *On the Town: A Community Adventure* by Judith Caseley and *Franklin's Neighborhood* by Paulette Bourgeois

Draw one "street" down the middle of the paper with a black marker. Add a few "side streets" if you wish. The streets should be wide enough for two of the toy cars to fit on, side by side. Depending on the ages and ability of the class, you may want to prepare some additional details of the town in advance.

Tape the butcher paper to the floor or a table. Have children gather around it for circle time. Tell children they are going to create their own town. Have children brainstorm for ideas for their town and then vote for their favorite. Draw a sign and write the name of the town on the paper. Repeat to name the streets (optional).

Provide children with crayons or markers, copies of the houses and other community buildings, as well as construction paper for making extra buildings.

Let's Create Our Town (continued)

Encourage children to work together to "plan" their community. Tell children that each of them will be able to select one house and one other type of building for the town. (If they decide as a group that their town needs more buildings, allow them to add as many as they feel they need.)

Encourage children to use the books provided for ideas as they consider the placement of buildings and the needs of the people in a town. Ask questions to encourage ideas.

Should the houses all be together?

What kinds of buildings does a community need?

Does the town need some types of buildings that are missing, like a barbershop?

Should there be a place set aside for parking?

After they decorate their homes and other buildings, have children place them on the butcher paper in the approximate places. When the locations are finalized, glue in place with glue sticks.

Encourage children to add more details such as sidewalks, driveways, street signs, parking lots, lawns, gardens, etc.

When the town is completed, allow children to use their town vehicles and action figures as they play in their very own town.

Extensions:

★ Let children vote for a "mayor for the day" for their town after talking about what qualities a person needs to be a town leader.

★ Let children suggest laws for their town. The group can vote on each suggestion and decide if it would be a good law for their town.

Write their laws on a sheet of paper.

63

1-57029-525-5 *Social Development Activities for Circle Time: Family and Community*

Home Patterns

64

1-57029-525-5 *Social Development Activities for Circle Time*
Family and Communit

Home Patterns

65

1-57029-525-5 *Social Development Activities for Circle Time:*
Family and Community

Red Light, Green Light

(Sing to the tune of "Twinkle, Twinkle Little Star")

Green light, green light, go, go, go.

Yellow, yellow, that means slow.

Red light, red light, stop, stop, stop.

If you don't believe it, ask your pop.

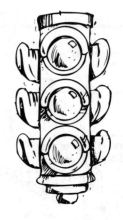

Why Do We Have Rules?

Children need to learn at an early age that people have responsibilities to get along with each other, to help each other, and to respect people and property. They must obey rules for their safety and the safety of other people.

Children are more likely to follow and respect rules if they know the purpose of the rules. These circle time questions encourage children to discuss rules.

Why are rules important?

Who must obey rules?

Do adults have to follow rules?

Do children and adults have to follow the same rules?

What is an example of a rule that only children must follow?

What if there were no rules?

Some Signs Mean "No"

Draw a large circle with a line through it on the board or chart paper. Ask children what it means? (The line through the circle means "NO" or "DO NOT." The picture inside the circle tells what we shouldn't do.)

Ask children to name some circle "NO!" signs they have seen and where they saw them. (No eating; no smoking; no crossing; no bike riding; no parking; don't pick the flowers; are a few of the common ones that will probably be familiar to children.)

Talk about why signs sometimes have pictures instead of words.

Singing the Rules

(Sing to the tune of "London Bridge")

Make a copy of the illustration at the bottom of this page and cut it out.

Introduce a unit on safety rules with this song. After each verse, stop and ask children why we have that rule. Then sing the verse a second time and invite them to join you.

Singing the Rules

Words

Buckle your seatbelt so you'll be safe,
You'll be safe; you'll be safe.
Buckle your seatbelt so you'll be safe
When riding in a car.

Stop! Look! Listen! so you'll be safe,
You'll be safe; you'll be safe.
Stop! Look! Listen! so you'll be safe
When you cross a street.

Don't jump around or make too much noise,
Make too much noise; make too much noise.
Don't jump around or make too much noise
When riding on the school bus.

Actions

(Hold up the seatbelt illustration. Imitate buckling a seatbelt.)

(Hold up the crossing guard illustration. Pretend to stop, look, and listen.)

(Hold up the school bus illustration. Pretend to drive a bus.)

Encourage children to suggest other rules to make more verses. Fill in the blanks with their ideas. Sing together.

_____ so you'll be safe,

You'll be safe; you'll be safe.

_____ so you'll be safe,

When _____.

Officer Sam Says

You will need:

★ *Officer Sam and Officer Samantha Patterns* cut out and colored (optional)
★ Two paint stirrers
★ Tape

Attach the two police officers to paint stirrers with tape to make puppets.

Model using the two puppets to state a rule (wear a helmet when you ride a bike) and the reason for the rule (so you don't hurt your head if you fall).

Ask: What is one rule you know that everyone must follow?

Hand one of the puppets to a child who volunteers. Ask that child to hold the puppet and say the rule.

Ask: Why is that a good rule?

Hand the other puppet to a child who volunteers. He can hold the puppet and explain why we have that rule?

Extensions:

★ Give each a copy of *Officer Sam and Officer Samantha Patterns* page to color.
★ Let children use the *Officer Sam and Officer Samantha Patterns* pages they colored as the cover for books they make about following rules. For each page they can draw themselves or others following rules. Help them write the words for the rules.
★ Help children write rules on colorful banners and decorate the banners with glitter, yarn, paints, crayons, and markers. Use the banners as room decorations.

---

68   1-57029-525-5 *Social Development Activities for Circle Time.*
Family and Community

Officer Sam and Officer Samantha Patterns

69

1-57029-525-5 *Social Development Activities for Circle Time: Family and Community*

Different Places, Different Rules

Homes, streets, parks, schools, playgrounds, malls, and swimming pools are places that may have their own rules. Rules can be different in different places.

Give children an example. At a swimming pool, the rule might be walk, don't run. That would be a good rule because the floor is wet and people could slip and fall if they ran. In a park or playground, running is fine.

Ask children to name one rule they know for each situation and the reason for that rule:

Riding in a car	Going to a movie	Riding a bicycle
Playing at a park	Shopping at the mall	Visiting the library
Playing in a sandbox	Riding a bicycle	Going to a zoo
Hiking in the woods	Driving a car	Visiting a grandparent

Catch Them Doing Something Right!

Provide positive reinforcement to children when you catch them doing something right.

You will need:

★ Copies of the *Catch Them Doing Something Right Award Certificates*

Note: You could make copies on colored paper so they stand out. If you use the same color paper such as gold for all awards, this will help make the awards recognizable and special.

Prepare the award certificates in advance by cutting them apart and writing in the child's name and specific rule followed. Date and sign it.

Use these certificates when you are working on a unit on following rules, learning safety rules, or anytime during the year when you want to reinforce good behavior.

Set aside a special circle time each day for handing out the certificates. (Waiting until the end of a week is much too long for very young children.) A good time would be shortly before dismissal. Make each child feel special as you hand out a certificate. Mention the child's achievement and shake his hand.

Catch Them Doing Something Right Award Certificates

Great Job!

Keep up the good work.

Date: _____

Awarded by: _____

_____

Date: _____

Awarded by: _____

way to go!

We're proud of you!

Atta Boy!

way to go!

_____

Date: _____

Awarded by: _____

Atta Girl!

Great Job!

_____

Date: _____

Awarded by: _____

1-57029-525-5 *Social Development Activities for Circle Time: Family and Community*

What Should You Do?

(Sing to the tune of "The Wheels on the Bus")

What Should You Do?

What should you do in an emergency?
Emergency? Emergency?
What should you do in an emergency?
First you must stay calm.

What should you do in an emergency?
Emergency? Emergency?
What should you do in an emergency?
Remember: Dial 911.

The Itsy Bitsy Spider

The itsy, bitsy spider
Had an emergency.
He called for help
Because he broke a leg, you see.

He reached for the phone
And he dialed 9-1-1.
Then the doctor came and helped him.
Now he's back playing in the sun.

Dial 911

You will need:

★ A realistic toy telephone (or use a real one that doesn't work anymore)

At circle time, talk about the word *emergency*.

What does it mean?
What is an emergency?
What should you do?

Reinforce the idea to children that they are not expected to handle emergencies alone. Role playing can help children avoid panic in real emergencies.

They must remember to remain calm and call for help. Tell children that if there is an emergency and no adult is nearby, they should dial 911 immediately. Pass the telephone around the circle. Ask each child to demonstrate how to dial 911.

Reassure children that if they call 911 by mistake, they will not be in trouble. It's better to be safe than sorry.

What Is an Emergency?

You will need:

★ Two realistic toy telephones

One at a time, hand a child a play telephone and keep one for yourself. Ask one of the "What-would-you-do?" questions listed or make up your own.

If it is an emergency, have the child dial 911 on the telephone. Pretend to answer the phone and carry on a dialog. Ask the nature of the emergency, the child's name, and where the child is located. This is the information they will need to provide in a real emergency. Praise children for remaining calm and responding correctly.

If a child thinks a situation is an emergency, but it's not, talk about why it isn't an emergency and what an appropriate response might be.

> What would you do if you saw smoke coming out of the neighbor's house? Is it an emergency?
>
> What would you do if you fell off your bike and scraped your knee or elbow and it hurt? Is it an emergency?
>
> What would you do if your big brother fell out of a tree and broke his arm when he was baby-sitting for you? Is it an emergency?
>
> What would you do if your big sister cut herself and there was lots of blood? Is it an emergency?
>
> What would you do if your mom fell down the stairs and couldn't get up? Is it an emergency?
>
> What would you do if your little brother got a piece of broken glass in his hand? Is it an emergency?
>
> What would you do if your dad had a sliver in his finger? Is it an emergency?
>
> What would you do if your friend was bitten by a mosquito? Is it an emergency?
>
> What would you do if you see a bat in your house? Is that an emergency?

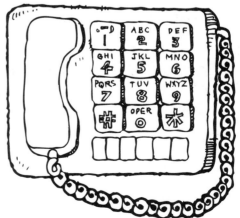

73

 # If You Were a Carpenter

This activity encourages children to learn about and create actions for various occupations.

Read each of the couplets. Have children make up actions for each verse.

If You Were a Carpenter

If you were a carpenter, you could build a house
For a dog, or a cat, or a person, or a mouse.

If you were a mechanic, you could fix a car.
You'd check the tires so we could drive far.

If you were a doctor, you'd make people well.
Instead of being sick, they'd soon feel swell.

If you were a baker, you'd make lots of bread
For Aaron, Anna, Anthony, and Uncle Fred.

If you were plumber, you could fix the tub
For my rubber duckie: rub-a-dub-dub.

If you were a farmer, you could grow corn and peas,
Pumpkins for Halloween, or maybe Christmas trees.

If you were a pilot, you could fly a plane
And take many people to Timbuktu or Spain.

If you were an astronaut, you'd explore the stars
And visit many planets, like Jupiter and Mars.

Encourage children to make up their own couplets with actions and share them with the group at circle time.

Goods or Services?

Tell children that some workers produce goods. Goods are things we use. Bakers make bread. Autoworkers build cars. Carpenters build houses. Ask children to name other workers who produce goods.

Tell children that some workers provide services we need, like barbers, doctors, and bankers. Ask children to brainstorm for other types of workers that provide services.

Mention many different types of occupations. (For ideas, use the "Occupations Pantomime Word List" on the next page.) Ask children to say whether that occupation involves producing goods or providing services.

Occupational Pantomimes

This activity helps children be more aware of the different jobs people in your community do every day. It takes many types of workers to produce the goods and services we use every day.

You will need:
★ A copy of "Occupational Pantomimes Word List"
★ A small bag or box

Cut apart the "Occupational Pantomimes Word List" on the next page. Select the ones you wish to use, add others of your own, and place them in a small paper bag or box.

When children are gathered for circle time, draw a slip of paper. Pantomime actions that imitate something a person with that occupation would do. Have the children guess what occupation you are pretending to do.

Remind children that *to pantomime* means "to show without using any words." (You may want to allow children to make sounds that would be appropriate for an occupation, such as blowing a horn.)

Children take turns drawing slips of paper. Whisper the word to the child so classmates cannot hear. Be certain the child knows what the word means.

Have the child pantomime actions for that occupation while the rest of the students guess. If students cannot guess, give them one or more clues. For example, if the occupation were banker and children could not guess it, you might say, "A person who does this job works with money every day."

Variation:
★ Children take turns drawing slips of paper with an occupation listed. Whisper the word to the child so classmates cannot hear. Be certain the child knows what the word means. Instead of pantomiming the occupation, the child gives a clue and the rest of the group guesses the occupation. The child can give a second or third clue if needed.

Occupational Pantomimes Word List

actor/actress	announcer	artist	astronaut
author	auto mechanic	baker	banker (bank worker)
barber/ beautician	baseball player	basketball player	builder
bus driver	carpenter	coach	cook (chef)
computer operator	computer fixer	cowboy/cowgirl	dentist
diver	doctor	farmer	firefighter
florist	football player	forest ranger	gardener
judge	lawyer	librarian	mail carrier
musician	news announcer	pilot	plumber
police officer	postal worker	singer	ski instructor
taxi driver	teacher	tennis player	train engineer
truck driver	veterinarian	waiter/waitress	zookeeper

Firefighters Are Community Workers

While teaching children about fire safety, include a field trip to a fire station if possible.

Read books to children about fire safety and what firefighters do. Talk about the equipment firefighters use and the special clothing they wear.

Give each child a firefighter hat. See directions at the bottom of the page for making these from newspaper in advance. As you sing this song to the tune of "London Bridge" children can put on their firefighter hats, then pretend to put on a coat, boots, and gloves.

What Does a Firefighter Wear?

A firefighter wears a helmet,
Wears a helmet, wears a helmet.
A firefighter wears a helmet
When she fights a fire.

A firefighter wears a coat,
Wears a coat, wears a coat.
A firefighter wears a coat
When he fights a fire.

A firefighter wears big boots,
Wears big boots, wears big boots.
A firefighter wears big boots
When she fights a fire.

A firefighter wears his gloves,
Wears his gloves, wears his gloves.
A firefighter wears his gloves
When he fights a fire.

Firefighter Hats

To make firefighter hats, fold newspaper as shown. Secure all loose edges with tape. If you'd like, let children color their hats red.

Cut badge shapes from yellow construction paper and tape it to the hats. Let children write a number or their names on the badges.

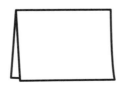 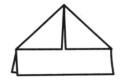   

1-57029-525-5 *Social Development Activities for Circle Time: Family and Community*

Who Would Use It?

You will need:

★ One copy of *Who Would Use It? Patterns*

★ Items depicting various occupations (Optional)

★ One copy of *What Job Would You Like?* for each student

Cut apart the illustrations on the *Who Would Use It? Patterns* page.

If desired, gather various other items that people in different occupations would use. Items could be used in place of or in addition to pictures.

At circle time, ask children to name jobs people do.

Show them the pictures or items, one at a time. Ask them to name the job or jobs someone might do who would use that item. Encourage children to realize that some items could be used by people in many different jobs. Ask them if someone in any other job might also use the same item. For example, a pencil and notepad could be used by a teacher, a doctor, a secretary, a judge, etc.

Extension 1: Invite parents or other people from the community to give short talks to the class about their jobs. Ask speakers to bring along one item they use regularly in their work.

Extension 2: Give each child drawing materials and a copy of *What Job Would You Like?*

Ask children to draw themselves doing a job they think they would like to do someday.

During circle time, ask children to take turns showing their drawings, telling what job they'd like to do, and giving one reason why they think they would like that job.

Display drawings for everyone to see.

This Is What I Want to Be

You will need:

★ Books from the "This Is What I Want to Be" series or other age-appropriate books depicting various occupations

Read a book to the children at circle time about what someone does for a job.

After you read, ask each child: Would you like to be a . . . (firefighter, doctor, bus driver . . .) someday? Ask child to give one reason why or why not.

Who Would Use It? Patterns

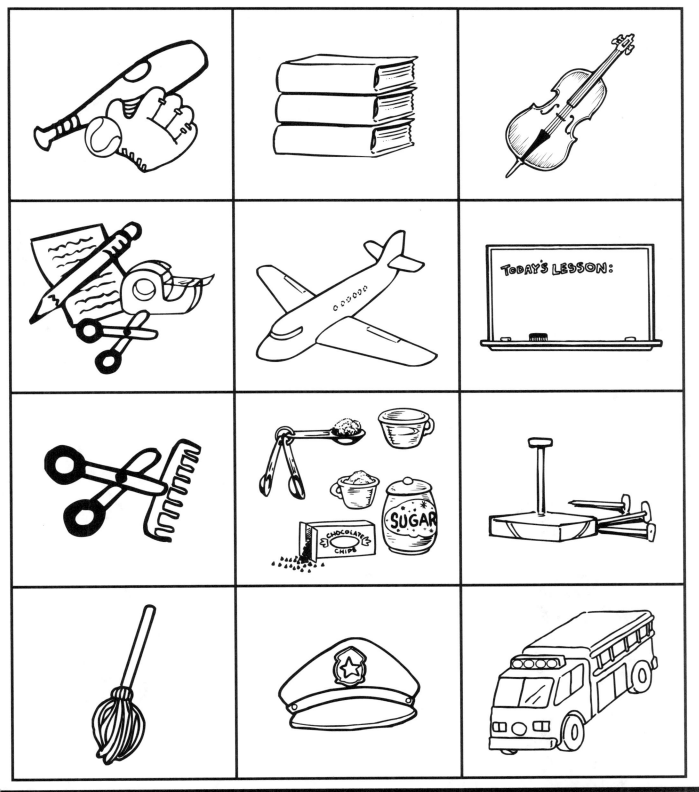

79

1-57029-525-5 *Social Development Activities for Circle Time: Family and Community*

What Job Would You Like?

80

1-57029-525-5 *Social Development Activities for Circle Time*
Family and Communit

Different Workers, Different Jobs

You will need:

★ *Ant Cities* by Arthur Dorros

As you read *Ant Cities* to the children at circle time, encourage them to notice what jobs the ants do and how the parts of the ant city are connected with tunnels. Stop and explain when you come to a new term to be certain children understand the word.

Remind children that people, like ants, do different jobs. Use the questions below as you read or after you finish the book.

Some ants build the ant city.

Ask: What kind of jobs do people do that are like the builder ants?

Some ants gather food, bring it to the ant city, prepare it, and store it.

Ask: Who gathers food for people?
Who prepares food for us to eat?
How does food get from where it's grown to us?

Some ants take care of the eggs, the larvae, and the pupae.

Ask: What jobs do people do that care for, teach, protect, and keep children healthy?

Some ants remove dirt and seed husks from the ant city to keep it clean.

Ask: What jobs do people do to keep our cities clean?

People Working Together

Reread *Ant Cities* to the children or spend a few minutes at the beginning of circle time reviewing what they learned.

From the book, we learned that "Ants work together to keep the whole ant city alive."

Introduce the word *cooperation*. Explain that *cooperation* means "to work together."

Ask questions to encourage children to talk about cooperation.

Why is working together important for ants?
Why is it important for people to work together?
Why is working together important for children?
What happens when people don't work together?

81

What Would You Do?

Role-playing and talking about everyday situations during circle time can help children think about in advance how they might handle similar situations. This can be an excellent way to help children see how they can take responsibility for their own actions.

Read the situations below one at a time or make up your own. For each situation, ask, "What would you do?" and "Why?"

Use the ideas over the course of two or more different circle time sessions to maintain children's interest.

Encourage children to take turns sharing their ideas and offering alternate ideas.

You accidentally rip a page in a library book.

You are playing baseball. The ball breaks a window.

You open a window. The wind blows over a pretty vase. It breaks.

You track mud on the floor. No one sees you do it.

You find an envelope with money in it.

Your dog gets loose. It digs up the neighbor's garden.

You find a great new pair of mittens on the playground.

Your friend doesn't want to play with you today.

You ate a whole package of cookies. Now you don't feel well.

Your sister got a new toy today. You didn't get one.

Your parents seem to be paying lots of attention to your new baby brother and none to you.

82

Looking at the Past

You will need:

★ A book that shows in pictures and words how people lived in the past, such as *Ox-Cart Man* by Donald Hall

★ Chart paper

★ Pencil or marker

Draw a line down the middle of the chart paper. Label one side "Then" and the other side, "Now." Prepare several pages ahead of time.

Read a book to the children at circle time that depicts everyday life in the United States in the past.

As you read, pause often. Encourage children to observe details of the illustrations such as the clothing people wore, what they ate, what they had in their homes, what the buildings looked like, what jobs they did, what children did for fun, and how they traveled from place to place.

Ask child to take turns naming things they learned about the past while reading the book. You may want to go back and show them the illustrations, page by page or reread selected sections.

Summarize what they say in a word or two and write it in the "Then" column. (Rode horses, No telephones, Log houses, Cornhusk dolls, etc.)

For each item in the "Then" column, ask children to describe how life is different today and write that in the "Now" column. (Ride in cars and planes, Have microwaves, Watch TV, etc.)

Repeat with other books about the past and add to the "Then" and "Now" list.

Extension:

★ Ask children to imagine living long ago and draw a picture of themselves showing how their life might have been if they had lived in the past.

★ Ask children to share their drawings with the class and explain how they thought their life might have been different.

83

Long, Long Ago

You will need:

★ A copy of *In the Past*, page 85

★ An old, battered suitcase or trunk (optional) filled with items to represent life in the past (if available)

Put items to represent life in the past in an old battered suitcase or trunk. Items can be real, like a 45 or 78 rpm record, a man's hat, or woman's bonnet, or replicas of old items. Check with your local historical society about borrowing several items that aren't too fragile. Place the suitcase in the middle of the circle.

Show children the illustrations from the *In the Past* page. You may want to cut them out so you can talk about them one at a time. For each item, ask children what they think it is and how people used it.

Ask children what they think you might have in the suitcase. Open the suitcase only a little bit and take out one item. Show it to the children. Help them figure out what it is and what it was used for.

For each picture or item, ask children what we use now instead for the same purpose.

Extension:

★ Take children on a field trip to an antique store or local history museum.

★ Children might enjoy looking through the pictures in a replica of an old Sears™ catalog.

What If?

Use "what if" questions to get children thinking about how everyday life was different for people in the past.

What if people didn't have cars, buses, trains, trucks, and airplanes? How would things be different if everyone walked or rode horses?

What if we didn't have any TVs, VCRs, or DVD players?

What if no one had electricity? What else wouldn't we have without electricity?

Tell children: We've talked about how many things were different in the past. People who live in the future will probably be very different too. What is one thing you think might be very different in the future?

In the Past

quill pen and ink bottle

wooden bucket

butter churn

wagon wheel

85

1-57029-525-5 *Social Development Activities for Circle Time: Family and Community*

 # Learning About Maps

Help children become familiar with maps, develop mapping skills, and demonstrate that they are members of a larger community.

You will need:

★ Colorful postcards from different places in your state: be sure to include one from your city
★ A large map of the state where you live
★ Colored pushpins—one needs to be larger or special in some way so it stands out from the others
★ Pieces of yarn in various sizes and colors

Place the state map on the floor in the middle of the group at circle time. Gather children around the state map. Explain that a map is a special kind of picture of a larger area.

Ask children to take turns telling what they observe about the map. (It shows where to find cities and roads, how to get from place to place, how far apart places are from each other, etc.)

Discuss the meaning of the different colors and symbols used on the map.

Ask children to name the city and state where they live.

Help them find their city on the map. Pin the map to the bulletin board.

Let one of the students put a pushpin on the map to mark your city. Use a pushpin that is unique in size or color to represent your city. Display the postcard of your city nearby and connect it to the pushpin on the map with a piece of colored yarn.

Show children postcards from other cities in your state. Talk about what the picture shows. Read the description of the place from the back of the postcard.

Find the matching cities on the map. Use direction words as you explain how to go from your city to the one on the postcards. Display postcards around the map. Connect postcards to pushpins on map with colored yarn.

We Live in the USA

You will need:

★ A large map of the USA showing each state

Place the large USA map in the center of the floor at circle time. Ask children if they know the name of our country. Tell them the name of our country is the United States of America. Sometimes we call it the USA for short.

The USA has 50 states. Ask them to name the state where they live. Help them find it on the map.

Say: "I have a friend who lives in . . . (name a state)" and point to it on the map. "Once I went on vacation to . . . (name a state)" and point to it on the map.

Ask children to take turns naming other states they know. Some might have lived in another state, gone there on a family vacation, or have friends and relatives in other states. Help them find each state.

50 States

You will need:

★ A USA map puzzle

Work together at circle time to make a USA map puzzle. As children put in the pieces, say the name of the states for them. Young children will need a puzzle that has the outline of each state clearly shown. Give hints to help them find where to put the pieces.

Symbols of the USA

You will need:

★ An American flag
★ Pictures of the Statue of Liberty, White House, US Capitol, and other patriotic symbols, which can be downloaded from the Internet

As children sit together at circle time, show them an American flag. Let them spend time examining the colors and shapes. Ask them what they think of when they see an American flag.

The flag is a symbol of our country. A symbol is something that makes us think of another place or idea. (You might use the example of the golden arches, which children associate with a specific fast-food restaurant.)

Voting Is a Privilege

Use these questions to begin a circle time discussion about voting.

What does voting mean?

Why do people vote?

What does *privilege* mean?

Why is voting a privilege?

What if we lived in a society where no one had a chance to help decide who should be the leader?

Extension:

★ Use this as an opportunity to familiarize children with the names of the current U.S. President and Vice President. Tell children that the President is elected by voters.

Take a Vote

Allow children the privilege of voting when appropriate. Here are some suggestions to use at circle time.

Offer children the opportunity to choose between two familiar books at reading time. Read the one that gets the most votes.

Offer children the choice from two circle time activities such as building with blocks or reading a story.

What Makes a Good Leader?

As an extension of a discussion on voting, ask children to brainstorm for ideas about what qualities a good leader needs. Encourage them to name people they know who they think are good leaders and give reasons why those people are good leaders.

Tie this in with a Presidents' Day activity.

Patriotism

During circle time, teach children several patriotic songs to reinforce the concept that we are all part of a larger community.

These sites provide words, additional verses, and/or music to many other patriotic songs:

http://www.niehs.nih.gov/kids/lyrics/cguard.htm
http://www.scoutsongs.com/categories/patriotic.html

America

by Rev. Samuel F. Smith

My country, 'tis of thee,
Sweet land of liberty,
Of thee I sing:
Land where my fathers died,
Land of the pilgrims' pride,
From every mountain side
Let freedom ring!

My native country, thee,
Land of the noble free,
Thy name I love:
I love thy rocks and rills,
Thy woods and templed hills;
My heart with rapture thrills
Like that above.

America the Beautiful

Words by Katharine Lee Bates
Melody by Samuel Ward

O beautiful for spacious skies,
For amber waves of grain,
For purple mountain majesties
Above the fruited plain!
America! America!
God shed His grace on thee,
And crown thy good with brotherhood
From sea to shining sea!

O beautiful for pilgrim feet,
Whose stern impassioned stress
A thoroughfare for freedom beat
Across the wilderness!
America! America!
God mend thine every flaw,
Confirm thy soul in self-control,
Thy liberty in law!

The Star-Spangled Banner

by Francis Scott Key

Oh! say, can you see, by the dawn's early light,
What so proudly we hailed at the twilight's last gleaming?
Whose broad stripes and bright stars, through the perilous fight,
O'er the ramparts we watched, were so gallantly streaming?
And the rockets' red glare, the bombs bursting in air,
Gave proof through the night that our flag was still there.
Oh! say, does that star-spangled banner yet wave
O'er the land of the free and the home of the brave?

A Globe Is a Special Kind of Map

You will need:

★ A globe

Have children gather around a globe. Talk about how the globe represents our planet, Earth. A globe is a small picture of what Earth would look like if you were in a rocket ship in space.

Ask: How is a globe like a flat map?

How is a globe different from a flat map?

What do the blue parts on the globe mean?

What part of the Earth is land?

Why are the land parts divided into different colored areas?

Where is the USA?

Let children take turns gently spinning the globe and pointing at random to a country. Read the name of the country selected. If you can, tell children one fact about the country, such as: An important city in France is Paris. It gets very cold in the winter in Norway. China is the largest country on Earth. Japan is a country made of up many islands. Canada is very close to the USA.

Our Global Family

You will need:

★ *Children Just Like Me* by Barnabas and Anabel Kindersley

Although the text of this book is too difficult for most preschoolers, they will enjoy the brightly colored illustrations of children from many countries. Use it as a starting point for different circle time activities.

Children can compare what they see the children in the pictures wearing and doing to what they wear and do.

If they are ready, help students find the countries where the children live on a world map or globe.

Use the illustrations as a starting point for talking about how even though we are different, in many ways we are the same, and we are all part of the global community.

1-57029-525-5 *Social Development Activities for Circle Time: Family and Community*

Earth: The Worldwide Community

You will need:

★ *Earthdance* by Joanne Ryder
★ Dolls and stuffed animals

As you share *Earthdance* with children at circle time, don't be surprised if they can't sit still. The lyrical text encourages listeners to become active participants. Encourage children to stand tall, stretch their arms out wide, and follow the motions in the text as you read. Let children dance their dolls or stuffed animals to "become" the Earth, to "dance in space," to spin and twirl gracefully, to "wiggle your shoulders" and "shake your hair." Dance together. It's a glorious day!

We share Earth with trees and flowers, sharks and elephants, whales and mice. We share Earth with billions of other people. When something happens in one part of the world, it can affect people all over the world. Good crops in one country can provide food for people in many countries.

Wouldn't it be great if everyone on Earth could be friends? What if everyone on Earth decided to dance together at the same time?

All living things—plants, animals, and people—depend on the Earth for food and water. Ask children:

How does an elephant depend on the Earth?

What do whales need to survive?

How do people depend on the Earth?

What do we need besides food and water?

What does the Earth provide for us?

What if people do not take care of the Earth?

If Earth becomes polluted, where will people and animals live?

Follow-Up Activity:

★ Read and discuss *The Wump World* by Bill Peet and/or *The Lorax* by Dr. Seuss with the children.

Recommended Books About Safety and Following Rules for Your Learning Center

Safety and Following Rules

Arthur's Fire Drill by Marc Tolon Brown

Bee Safe by Charles Reasoner

The Berenstain Bears Learn About Strangers by Stan and Jan Berenstain

Dinosaurs, Beware: A Safety Guide by Marc Brown and Stephen Krensky

Don't Talk to Strangers by Kevi

Emergency! by Margaret Mayo

Fire! Fire! by Gail Gibbons

Fireman's Safety Hints (Barrons Educational Series)

Fire Safety by Pati Myers Gross

Franklin's Bicycle Helmet by Eva Moore

I Can Be Safe by Pat Thomas

It's Time to Call 911 by Penton Overseas

Peanut's Emergency by Christina Solat

No Dragon for Tea: Fire Safety for Kids (And Dragons) by Jean Pendzuol

Officer Buckle and Gloria by Peggy Rathmann

Oh No, Nicky by Harriet Ziefert

Safety First Please! and It Won't Make You Sneeze by Robert Bemardini

Sergeant Murphy's Traffic Book by Richard Scarry

Stop, Drop, and Roll by Margery Cuyler

Stranger Safety by Pati Myers Gross

Who Is a Stranger and What Should I Do? by Linda Walvoord Girard

Yes, No, Little Hippo by Jane Belk Mancure

Prop Box Suggestions

Toy emergency and rescue vehicles

Play telephones (or real ones that don't work anymore)

Handmade stop signs, school crossing signs, and other types of traffic signs

Firefighters hats

Stop! Drop! Roll!

Hold circle time outside in the grass or in the gym on gym mats, so children can practice the Stop, Drop, and Roll technique.

Explain the rule: If your hair or clothes catch on fire, don't run.

Explain why: Running will make the fire worse.

What to do: Remember these three steps: Stop! Drop! Roll!

Stop!
Drop to the ground!
Roll to put out the fire!

Encourage children to actively practice these three steps as you call out, "Stop! Drop! Roll!"

Who Is a Stranger?

Most young children are open and friendly. They trust adults. Unfortunately, not all adults can be trusted. As educators of young children, we can help children learn to be cautious around strangers.

Use your own words to explain the concept below for a discussion about strangers during circle time.

A stranger is someone we don't know well. We have met many strangers already. Some have become friends. There are strangers in our neighborhood, at stores, and at school. Even people we see often, but don't really know are strangers, like the mail carrier, the school bus driver, or the clerk at the store. Most strangers are nice people. They are helpful and friendly.

Some strangers are not good people. They may want to hurt a child or take him away from his parents. They may want to touch a child in ways that are not proper. Strangers don't become friends just by acting friendly for a few minutes.

Bad people do not always look mean or bad. They can seem to be friendly. They can be men or women, young or old. They can be dressed in old grubby clothes or in brand-new fancy ones.

Rules About Strangers

Circle time is a good time to talk with young children about scary situations because it is a secure environment. You may suggest children bring a favorite doll or stuffed animal with them.

Talk about the three stranger safety rules, the reasons why we have those rules, and what to do. Reinforce each by asking, "What should you do . . .?" and encouraging children to reply, "Shout NO! and run away!"

The rule: Never ride or walk anywhere with ANYONE, unless your parents have told you ahead of time that it's OK.

The reason: Some strangers may try to hurt children.

What to do: Shout NO! and run away.

Ask: "What should you do if a stranger asks you to go for ride on his shiny new motorcycle?" (Children reply: "Shout NO! and run away.")

The rule: Never leave a building, like a store, school, or library, with a stranger.

The reason: Some strangers may try to take children away from their parents.

What to do: Shout NO! and run away.

Ask: "What should you do if a stranger asks you to leave the library and go outside with her?" (Children reply: "Shout NO! and run away.")

The rule: Never accept gifts or money from strangers.

The reasons: Some bad people try to trick children by offering them gifts or money.

What to do: Shout NO! and run away.

Ask: "What should you do if a stranger offers to give you money or a gift?" (Children reply: "Shout NO! and run away.")

Explain to children they should not run off by themselves or try to hide in a place where there are no people. They should run to a place where there are MANY people, such as a restaurant or gas station. They could run to the home of someone they know well if it is close. They should make a lot of noise because noise attracts attention. A bad stranger will not want anyone to see him or her. Making a lot of noise is good.

1-57029-525-5 *Social Development Activities for Circle Tim
Family and Communi*

 # Role Play: What Should You Do? (Part 1)

Help children learn more about dealing with strangers through role-playing. At circle time, describe one of the scenarios listed or make up your own. You could get another adult or older child to help act it out. Use no more than one or two during any one circle time. Let children discuss what they should do. A suggestion for appropriate action is included for each situation.

1. A man who looks like a pro football player stops you on the playground and asks you questions, like: What is your name? Where do you live? He looks a lot like your favorite football player. Maybe he'll give you his autograph.

   Is he a stranger? What should you do?

   He is a stranger. Do not answer any questions about yourself. Get away from him fast. Go to a place where there are other people.

2. You and your best friend are walking to the park. A woman asks if the two of you would like to go with her to see a movie . . . (name a movie that is currently popular). She says she will buy popcorn and soda for you both.

   Is she a stranger? What should you do?

   She is a stranger. Shout, NO! Do not go ANYWHERE with her, even though you are with a friend. Leave the area immediately. Go to a place where there are other people. Tell an adult what happened. Never go anywhere with a stranger no matter what he or she says or offers you.

3. A man who looks a lot like your grandfather tells you he is lost. He asks you to walk with him to the corner of Second and Maple Streets, which is a few blocks away.

   Is he a stranger? What should you do?

   He is a stranger. Do not go ANYWHERE with him. If there are other people around, you could ask someone else to help the man. If no one else is around, stay away from the man. Tell him you are sorry, but you aren't allowed to do that. Most adults ask other adults for help, not children.

 # Role Play: What Should You Do? (Part 2)

4. A lady comes to your door and says, "Will you come with me and help me find my dog if I give you $10? I know my poor little dog is so scared." She starts to cry. You mom is in the shower, and you are the only other one home.

   Is she a stranger? What should you do?

   > She is a stranger. You should not go ANYWHERE with her. Close the door and lock it. Call loudly to get your mother's attention. This woman is not acting right. Most adults will not offer money to children. They will ask other adults to help.

5. A man calls out from an alley and asks for your help. He looks like he is bleeding.

   Is he a stranger? What should you do?

   > He is a stranger. Do not go close to him. He may be pretending. Call loudly for help. Get another adult to help. Use the nearest telephone and call 911.

6. A man about 20 in a fancy red convertible stops his car in front of your house and asks you for directions to the park.

   Is he a stranger? What should you do?

   > He is a stranger. Do not go near the car. Usually adults ask other adults for directions, not children. Go in your house and tell an adult.

7. You're shopping with your grandma at a large store. You wander off to the toy aisle. A man in a store uniform comes up to you and says, "Hurry, your grandma fell and broke her leg. The ambulance took her to the hospital. I'll take you there."

   Is he a stranger? What should you do?

   > He is a stranger. Do not go with him. How would he know who your grandma was? If she really did have a broken leg, someone would make an announcement for you to come to the front desk. Go to the front desk and find out if anything really did happen to your grandma. They will find her for you.

It's best if you stay with your parents or other adult when shopping. If you do wander off alone, do not leave the store or go somewhere else in the store with a stranger.